The Popular Training Series From
Practical Horseman

Build a Better Athlete!

16 Gymnastic Exercises for Your Horse

By Leslie Webb

Produced by the editors of
***Practical Horseman* Magazine**

First Published in 2006 by PRIMEDIA Equine Network
656 Quince Orchard Road, #600
Gaithersburg, MD 20878
301-977-3900

VP, Group Publishing Director: Susan Harding
Editorial Director: Cathy Laws
Director, Product Marketing: Julie Beaulieu

Printed in the USA.

Practical Horseman
Editor: Sandy Oliynyk
Senior Editor: Kip Goldreyer
Consulting Editor: Deborah Lyons
Art Director: Alyssa Tavernia

Book Editor: Sue M. Copeland
Photographer: Tass Jones
Book Design: Lauryl Suire Eddlemon
Production: Lara Pinson

*The author wishes to thank Harmony Sporthorses, owner of Harmony's Cassiano and Harmony's Picasso,
and Riitta Saada, owner of Montero V.*

Order by calling 800-952-5813 or online at www.HorseBooksEtc.com

Library of Congress Cataloging-in-Publication Data

Webb, Leslie.
  Build a better athlete : 16 gymnastic exercises for your horse / by Leslie
Webb and the editors of Practical Horseman.
     p. cm.
  ISBN-13: 978-1-929164-34-9
  ISBN-10: 1-929164-34-3
  1. Horses--Training. 2. Horses--Exercise. I. Practical Horseman. II.
Title.
  SF287.W42 2006
  636.1'0835--dc22

                         2006028989
                          Rev.

CONTENTS

POSITION CHECK

Learn how my gymnastics program will bring out the athlete in your horse. Then review your position so you'll maximize my program's benefit.

I am riding Picasso in a classic dressage position, a vertical line running from my shoulder through my hip and down to my heel. There is a straight line from my elbow through my forearm and reins to Picasso's mouth.

ARE YOU LIKE MANY OF THE students I meet during clinics—you've got all the energy and desire in the world, but your training program is a little hit-or-miss? Are you baffled by trying to feel and reproduce the abstract terms we dressage folk so casually throw around, such as through the back, self-carriage, follow the motion, in front of the leg, and roundness?

And, yes, although you know our dressage tests are a "blueprint" for training your horse, do you find you're missing some tools and equipment when you try to follow the blueprint and produce a finished product?

Well, that's a shame, because …

You Have an Athlete There

Your horse may never go to the Olympics but he's doing a sport, and he should have the best possible chance of using his body correctly and well. (This not only improves his performance but has been shown to reduce unnecessary injuries.)

That's why in this book I'm going to share the progressive system I've developed to "gymnasticize" my horses: to balance, supple, straighten, and strengthen them, whether they're green youngsters just starting their careers or advanced horses from Europe. (Many such horses, though they know such "tricks" as tempi changes and canter pirouettes, can't do something as basic as cantering in a straight line off the rail!)

This system is based on a progressive series of gymnastics using common maneuvers and figures: straight lines, circles, transitions, turns on the forehand, squares, diamonds, and octagons. You'll guide your horse through these exercises the way a personal trainer guides you around the different weights, machines, and circuits at the gym.

I think you'll like the system. Rather than beginning with dressage movements and trying to use them to create qualities the tests require, such as balance, thrust, collection, and straightness, you'll start with simple exercises and build your horse into an athlete who can willingly, comfortably, even expressively do any job—including a terrific dressage test.

Not Just for Dressage

Any horse can benefit from gymnasticizing, whether he's a hunter, eventer, jumper, trail, or eq horse. (Believe me, as the competition heats up in the equitation division, more and more eq riders are coming to me and my fellow dressage trainers for flat lessons!)

In fact, the name of your sport isn't the point. What is? Teaching your horse in a fun, doable, understandable way to listen and respond to your seat, to bend equally in both directions from poll to tail, to go forward and come back smoothly in response to the lightest of aids, and to stay balanced when he turns.

How do gymnastic exercises do all that? By being …

■ **Simple (note: I didn't say "easy").** They allow you and your horse to focus on and fully develop one skill at a time. Even if he's working at an advanced level, holes in his training may be slowing him down; I'll show you when and how a pattern can identify and fill them.

■ **Systematic.** Each pattern logically builds on the patterns that came before it and, in turn, becomes a building block for the patterns that come after. You don't progress to the next exercise until you've got the skills for this one under your belt. And if you find that you're still having trouble—let's say your horse is having an

A Bit About Tack

■ **Be a fit fanatic.** Make sure your saddle fits and is properly balanced. (If you don't know how, ask your trainer or a qualified saddler.) And if you've got a young horse, remember that as he grows, matures, and muscles up, his shape will change. Have his saddle checked at least every six months.

■ **Adjust your stirrup length.** With your foot out of the stirrup and your leg relaxed and hanging down, the bottom of the iron should rest about an inch above the bottom of your heel. (If you're a hunter rider, the bottom of the iron should be about level with your ankle bone.) In most cases, this will allow you to drop your heel down for maximum security and contact and create a definite knee-angle "hinge" for flexibility and the ability to absorb your horse's motion. If you're standing on tiptoe, your stirrups are too long for security; you have to depend on your heel alone to give leg aids to your horse. But your heel alone can't get him to step further

underneath himself (your inside seat bone and thigh do that) or straighten his body or press him around a figure (your outside seat bone and thigh do that).

■ **Spurs? Maybe later.** I wear spurs once a week with my upper-level horses because FEI competition requires spurs. The rest of the time I school without them. That way they don't lull me into relying on them instead of making my horses sensitive and responsive to my seat and leg—one of the very basic skills you and I are going to work on in this book. Spurs also keep me from applying one of my favorite wake-up calls when a horse isn't listening: a little thump with my heel. Finally, if you don't have complete control over your leg, spurs can inadvertently poke your horse and send him all sorts of unintentionally mixed messages. Instead of spurs, I recommend you …

■ **Use a dressage whip.** I call this "my little helper." You'll use it to reinforce your leg aids. But remember it's

only for reminding, never for punishing or for using as an aid in its own right.

■ **Be bit smart.** I like a plain medium-thick French schooling snaffle—it's a nice bit that seems to suit most horses.

■ **And get yourself a bucking strap.** My mentor, former US Olympic coach Erich Bubbel, who came to this country with a classical East Prussian equestrian education, taught me to use a bucking strap when I was riding the Trakehner stallion Pregelstrand. That strap really came in handy when I started training Pregelstrand's son, Titan—because whenever he wanted to do his thing, I could put him on a 20-meter circle and loop the thumb of my inside hand around the bucking strap. He couldn't jerk the rein away from me or escape the bend. My hand stayed still (so I wasn't adding fuel to the fire by inadvertently jerking on his mouth). And I could pull myself just deep enough into the saddle to be secure and safe.

"equine moment" understanding leg-yield—you can easily back up a step to the previous lesson (turn on the forehand in leg-yield position) and "explain" away his confusion. Rather than drilling or punishing him—which never works—you clearly and simply solve the problem by correcting the underlying issue.

> Nothing about these exercises interferes with or puts on hold whatever you're already doing with your horse. Go right ahead and ride and compete as you have been doing.

■ **Diagnostic.** Because you work them in both directions, the exercises serve as an early-warning system for weakness, soreness, and resistance.

■ **Sensitizing.** Your horse will learn to tune in to your seat for subtle cues that increase communication and response, determine his direction and bend, and act as the metronome that sets his rhythm, tempo, and length of stride.

■ **Useful.** As you work your way through the lessons, they'll help you develop a skill that's missing from many an amateur rider's toolbox: a logical, systematic warm-up and schooling program that you can use every time you ride or compete.

■ **A light bulb!** The simple act of guiding your horse through these gymnastics almost automatically puts him on the aids and makes him rhythmic, supple, and balanced. This in turn gives concrete shape and feel to those pesky abstract concepts I mentioned, such as "through the back." (To me this simply means the horse is listening and responding to your seat and minute changes in your balance. The more sensitive he is to seat and balance, the more through the back he is. But if you go to use your seat and get no response, even if he's very forward and maybe "on the bit," he's a horse that's NOT through the back.)

Here's What We'll Do

In each chapter I'll give you one gymnastic exercise. I'll explain what it's intended to accomplish and why. I'll describe in detail and illustrate with photos exactly how to do it, what it should feel like, and what problems to avoid. I'll dig into your position and the timing of your aids—including the all-important half-halt (which, believe me, is far less complicated than many of us are led to believe). And I'll explain how the exercise can correct an

underlying problem that may be hindering you and your horse in the show ring.

Best of all, nothing about these exercises interferes with or puts on hold whatever you're already doing with your horse. Go right ahead and ride and compete as you have been doing. As you work your way "around the gym" chapter after chapter, you can just neatly and seamlessly incorporate into your regular work the improved qualities and skills that the lessons will create.

Sound good? Great! In this chapter let's start with that basic of basics: the most effective, useful, secure, and attractive dressage position possible, with a secure lower leg to support your upper body so you don't need to rely on the reins for balance. (If you ride over fences, by all means keep reading, but continue to rely on your hunter/jumper position. I'm not here to change what works for you in your sport—and, with a few small differences, is pretty much the same in both sports.)

Establish Your Position

Sit with the classic straight line from shoulder to hip to heel, and with your shoulder tall but relaxed (which is where a long, secure leg really starts). If there's a seam on the side of your breeches, make sure it (or an imaginary line if you don't have a seam) stays vertical from waist to seat and you'll automatically eliminate such common position problems as perching on your crotch, falling behind the motion, stiffening and hollowing your back in an attempt to sit straight and tall, or collapsing in your middle and rolling onto your back pockets.

Because your upper body tends to influence your horse's shoulders and forehand (and you really steer his forehand, not his nose), keep your shoulders perpendicular to the track and your chest "looking" where you want him to go.

Allow your upper arm to hang softly vertical by your side and your forearm to be part of a straight line from elbow to hand to bit. Close your fingers firmly on the reins and hold your hands with your thumbs up but slightly tilted in toward each other. (A good "rule of thumb": If the backs of your hands have the same angle as your horse's shoulders, they will automatically have the most correct, effective position and the best distance apart.) For now, keep a loose or light following contact— what I call "eavesdropping on your horse"—without worrying or fussing at him about where he's putting his head.

Roll your thigh and knee into the saddle so you feel a relaxed and firm contact—not clamped or pinching—from your seat bones through your thigh to your knee and partway down your calf. Point your toe almost straight ahead and, without forcing, keep your weight down in your deep heel. Because your seat and legs influence your horse's hindquarters, sit square and straight in the saddle with your hips perpendicular to the track but with a penny's worth more weight on your inside seat bone. Position your inside leg at the girth and your outside leg—from the hip, not just from the knee—a penny's worth behind the girth. For now, and in general, keep your shoulders and hips parallel. (We'll do some lateral movements in the future where his forehand and haunches will track differently; for those, you'll use your shoulders and hips in a slightly "unparallel" way.)

Position Check (and Fix)

My students know that at any time during a lesson— at the halt, walking, trotting, cantering, even doing a leg-yield—I'll have them test and in some cases correct their positions by getting up in what I call "the dreaded dressage two-point." That's the up-phase of the posting trot, where I want to see them balance without relying on the horse's mouth, follow his motion, and effectively use their aids while keeping their heels deep, their seat bones close to the saddle but not relying on it for support, and their hips and knees working as shock absorbers. (Hunter/jumper riders have known forever the value of two-point: It not only shines a light on position weaknesses; it fixes them!)

So go ahead and try it. If you fall back, the bad news is that you probably ride in a "chair seat," with your leg out in front of you. If you tip forward, you probably ride perched, with your leg too far back. Here's the good news (in either case): Two-point can fix you! Grasp a bit of mane for security if you need to, and get up in two-point, your weight deep in your heel and your knee softly flexible. Practice this position—which also, incidentally, strengthens your back—until you feel as if you could comfortably ride that way in any gait, all day. That's when you know you've got a good position with your leg underneath you. And then you'll be ready for Chapter 2: Using your seat to go forward and back.

1 My head is sitting squarely on top of my shoulders, and there's a straight line from my shoulder to my hip to my heel. When I first saw this photo I thought my stirrup leather was too far behind the girth (it's clearly a bit behind the vertical), but I've concluded that this appearance is a result of this particular saddle's design, and is less significant than the fact that the saddle—which is well-balanced on Picasso's back—allows me to maintain a good shoulder-hip-heel alignment. Because my thigh is part of my seat, I've rolled it and my knee into the saddle for a firm but relaxed continuous contact from my seat bone down through my knee and …

2 … partway down my calf, where the power comes from when I ask my horse to go forward. The ball of my foot is firmly centered on the stirrup iron for security and balance, my toe is pointed just forward enough for the iron to be perpendicular to Picasso's side, and I have plenty of weight in my heel without forcing or driving it down. (Doing so would tend to be counterproductive because it would pull my knee and thigh away from the saddle.)

3 I'm square and centered in the saddle (which makes the saddle sit square and centered on Picasso). My head is right there in the middle of my shoulders, and my shoulders and hips are level and parallel with each other (although you'll notice that my right shoulder is ever-so-slightly lower than the left; that's because of an old injury). My elbows are by my sides.

4 My upper arm is vertical and close to my side, and there's enough angle in my elbow to create a straight line to my hands and the bit. My hands are right in front of the pommel, above Picasso's withers, and tilted just enough to mimic the angle of his shoulders. (If you held a yardstick flat against his shoulder, it would rest on the back of my hand.)

5 With my leg relaxed and hanging down, the bottom of my stirrup iron is about an inch above the bottom of my heel, so …

6 … when I pick up my stirrups, I have weight in my heel and nice shock-absorbing angles in front of my hip and behind my knee. Note that although I don't have a side seam on these breeches, the little dart by my waist is pretty much vertical. This means I'm balanced properly on my seat bones: neither collapsed and rolled back on my pockets and behind the motion (the top of the dart would tilt back) nor arched, perched on my crotch, and ahead of the motion (the top of the dart would tilt forward).

7 My bucking strap is long enough for me to get a thumb around it but short enough that it's not sticking up above the pommel of my saddle. Bucking straps are legal in the competition arena, even through FEI levels. And despite what some people say, bucking straps aren't just for wimps. Look closely at some of the top dressage riders in the world and you'll see bucking straps discreetly attached to the D-rings on their saddles.

RIGHT

WRONG

Rider Position

Two-Point Position

RIGHT: At the walk, I check to make sure I'm balanced and secure by assuming a dressage two-point position: the highest point of the up-phase of my posting trot. My elbows could be a little closer to my body, but my thigh and knee are rolled securely into the saddle, I have contact down through the middle of my calf, and my knee and hip joints have plenty of shock-absorbing angle. Although my heel isn't as deep as a hunter rider's would be, there's definitely weight in it.

Even though I've got long, loopy reins, if I had contact there would be a nice straight line from my elbow to my hand to the bit. And for now that long, loopy rein confirms that I'm not relying on Picasso's mouth for balance. In fact, his low head, long stride (look how his right hind is reaching all the way up underneath me), and contented look tell me loud and clear that he's completely comfortable with my position; we're relaxed and in sync with each other.

WRONG: I'm perched high above the pommel (and ahead of the motion), I'm standing on my toes, my knee and hip angles are straight, and my back is stiff and arched. Picasso is clearly not happy with this state of affairs. He's raised his head and hollowed his back in protest. And I'm so insecure that if he were to slam on the brakes, I could fly over his head.

CHAPTER 1

GYMNASTIC EXERCISE 1:
FORWARD AND BACK

Use your seat to start
teaching your horse to
communicate and respond
"through" his back.

With the correct rider position, I am lengthening and shortening Picasso's stride
with just the push in my seat.

LET'S GET RIGHT DOWN TO THE fun of gymnasticizing your horse by developing his longitudinal flexibility: his ability to lengthen and shorten his stride instantly and responsively. You'll create this "accordion-like" response by using your seat (and when I say "seat," I mean buttocks, seat bones, and thighs) as a metronome that tells him how long or short his stride should be. Longer pushes—I'll tell you how to "push" in a moment—mean longer strides. Shorter pushes mean shorter strides.

Longitudinal flexibility is useful for hunters, jumpers, and three-day horses (think of moving up in a line or coming back to negotiate a cross-country obstacle after a gallop), but it's vital in dressage. For example, free walk always has a double coefficient; you're just throwing away points if you can't show a good free walk in which your horse lowers and stretches his head and neck and covers as much ground as possible.

Forward and back in response to your seat is the first tiny baby step on the way toward lengthening (which

you need to show starting at First Level); the same applies to collection and extension. And even though you may never get to Grand Prix and need to show piaffe and passage, at any level you want to have the instantaneous forward-and-back effect that those movements require to the max.

Here's What You'll Do
You'll ride at the walk on a straight line, on a long or loose contact. In this exercise pattern, you'll go from a medium walk, in which your horse's hind feet touch the ground in or slightly in front of the prints of his forefeet,

Forward and Back

Lengthen your horse's walk steps with your seat and leg. Then shorten the push in your seat to shorten the steps in the walk.

to a freer walk in which he stretches, covers more ground, and takes longer strides (the longer the better) with his hind feet clearly touching the ground in front of the prints of his forefeet. Then you'll smoothly return to a medium walk.

Why am I asking you to walk on a loose or long rein? First, to encourage you to make your seat aids effective. Second, to avoid the considerable risk of ruining your horse's walk by prematurely trying to pull him together. Not only can doing so rob him of drive, relaxation, and freedom; in the worst-case scenario, it could encourage him to pace, moving lateral pairs of legs forward simultaneously or nearly so. That's a faulty gait for any English-riding sport.

One of the neatest features about this gymnastic is that it's mentally and physically stress-free. That's why it's one of the first exercises I do with a young horse I'm starting or any horse I'm bringing back from an injury. In fact, it's what all training should be: fun. It engages your horse's brain cells by making him focus and think about what you want, but it's straightforward enough that he's not going to worry or get confused. It's also something you can do anywhere, at any time. In fact, I encourage you to take it out of the arena and onto the trail. Just wait until you and your horse challenge a trail buddy to a walking race—and win!

Before we start, I want to tell you why …

Timing Is Everything

I'm going to talk a lot about timing as we work our way through these gymnastics. To me timing simply means giving an aid, a half-halt, or a correction when it's most likely to have the greatest effect. In this gymnastic, for example, the most influential time to ask your horse to make a longer stride by stepping a hind foot more energetically forward and farther underneath him is when that foot lifts off the ground and begins its flight forward. The worst—or least effective—time, and the one most likely to send him mixed messages and cause confusion, is when his foot has completed its flight forward and is arriving at or already on the ground, so that it literally has nowhere to go.

Because the walk consists of four predictably consecutive steps—left hind, left fore, right hind, right fore—you can figure out when to encourage and activate a hind foot by:

- **Glancing down.** Check your horse's shoulder (without dropping your chin, tipping your head, or leaning over, which will just unbalance the two of you). When you see or feel his left shoulder swing forward (and, with it, his left foot), the very next foot to lift off the ground and come forward will be his right hind.
- **Feeling the movement of his rib cage.** When it swings left (you'll feel it push your left leg out a bit), his right hind is stepping forward. When it swings right (and pushes against your right leg), his left hind is stepping forward.
- **Feeling his back.** This is more subtle than the other two signs. His back will drop a bit on the right when his right hind is coming forward; his back will drop on the left when his left hind is coming forward.
- **Recruiting a friend.** Have a friend call out to you "right, left, right, left," in time with your horse's hind legs until you have the feel of them.

Check my "Tips for Good Training" at right. Then let's …

Make Normal Strides

Pick up a nice, energetic marching walk on a loose or long passive contact. Sit square in the saddle, with your shoulders and hips perpendicular to the track your horse is on and your weight evenly distributed on both seat bones and in both stirrups. Help him travel straight by imagining that twin beams of light are shooting out like lasers from your hip bones, past his neck and head, and that his path lies directly between those beams.

Now ask your horse to lengthen his stride. Stretch your torso up so you very slightly increase the downward pressure of your seat bones, increasing your communication with him. (It may be slight, but believe me, your horse will feel it—and the more you gymnasticize him, the more sensitive and responsive to such tiny adjustments and cues he'll become.) Each time he lifts a hind leg off the ground, smoothly and rhythmically use your seat to give a push forward that asks him to take a longer step and reach farther underneath himself. You should feel him get longer, looser, and swingier under you in response.

OK, I can just hear you saying, "Yes, Leslie, but HOW do I push?" To me, the motion is exactly the same sort of "scoop" that you made with your seat as a kid on a swing when you wanted the swing to go higher. Some trainers describe this pushing movement as "polishing" the saddle with your breeches, or sitting on the front edge of a stool and using your seat to tip the stool forward so the back legs come off the floor. Whichever of these images works for you, keep your butt muscles relaxed as you push; don't tighten them. (Go ahead and tighten them right now, while you're sitting and reading this, and you'll feel how tightening will squeeze your seat bones away from the saddle instead of allowing them to settle down around it. An effective seat comes from sitting "into" your horse, not hovering "on top of" him.)

Keep your knees and thighs relaxed as well. Gripping or pinching will actually block your horse and tell him not to come forward (and will prevent you from using your lower leg effectively, should you need it).

Keep your upper body vertical. If you perch or tip forward in an effort to help your horse make bigger strides, your seat bones will slide to the rear and he'll feel a backward push. If you sit back on your pockets in an effort to drive him, your seat bones will slide forward and he'll feel you fall behind his center of gravity; mentally, you may be telling him to go forward, but your body language will be shouting, "Slow down and get hollow." (This effect came home to me loud and clear when my son, Tyler, was a toddler. Carrying him on my shoulders, I could go forever if he sat up; if he leaned back, I could barely stand, let alone keep walking.)

Tips for Good Training

■ **Get off the rail.** When your horse hugs the rail, he's following his own agenda. He's doing his own steering. He's not tuned in to you. And in all likelihood he's a bit crooked. Because his hindquarters are wider than his forehand, when his outside fore and outside hind are glued to the rail, his inside hind is farther into the arena than his inside fore, which means his spine is slightly curved in and he's not straight. Avoid this problem by riding on the second track or third track (one or two horse-widths into the arena), the centerline, the diagonal, or the quarterline. (Doing so may be a bit challenging; you'll discover just how "addicted" to the rail your horse has become and what a magnetic pull it exerts over him.)

■ **Not all pushes are created equal.** I think of them as on a scale of 1 to 10, or like the volume on a radio. When you're first teaching your horse to listen to your seat, you may have to turn up the volume to 8 or 9—long, strong pushes that clearly tell him what you want. Once he responds, you can turn the volume down to 2 or 3 and just "coast" or follow along with his motion. If he makes a mistake, you may have to correct him by turning the volume back up to 6 or 7.

Play with this idea, but always with the goal of turning down the volume until your aids are as quiet as possible. As my mentor, Erich Bubbel, used to say, "If a horse can feel a fly on his side, he can feel the lightest of aids." When your horse responds to a "fly weight" aid, you'll never want to use heavier, rougher, or more obvious ones again. And he will truly achieve the goal of dressage by giving the impression of doing what's required of him of his own accord.

■ **You are the teacher.** Every time you put your foot in the stirrup and swing a leg over your horse, his training begins right then and there, not just when you get to the arena. For example, don't let him get away with a pokey, lazy walk from the mounting block to the arena but then punish him for not marching out once you get inside the gate. To do so is confusing and unfair to him.

Rights ...

1 Here you see a relaxed, obedient, nearly perfect free walk. Picasso's right hind is stepping well in front of the footprint of his right fore (which you can't see, unfortunately) in response to longer pushes from my seat. This is a quiet, composed picture, isn't it? I have a straight line from my elbow to the bit and a long, passive, following contact with his mouth. My shoulders and hips are perpendicular to the straight track he's following. (We're on the second track—a horse-width into the arena—so he doesn't have the rail to lean on.)

Having just felt his rib cage move to the left as his right hind stepped forward, I'm about to feel his rib cage move right as his left hind lifts and steps forward. What you can't see in a still photograph is my seat

making nice, long pushes to encourage nice, long, energetic strides. What you can see clearly is that his topline neck muscles are working—which is great!

2 As I shorten the pushes in my seat, Picasso shortens his stride so his left hind steps just slightly over the footprint of his left fore. My body position is unchanged except that I may be sitting up a bit more, which serves to increase the slight downward weighting—and so the influence—of my seat bones. Note that throughout this series of photos, my lower leg remains very quiet. This gymnastic is all about communicating through my horse's back with my seat—buttocks, seat bones, and thighs—and not my lower leg. Like all

my gymnastics, it is also not a drill or a grind. Just look at Picasso; he'll tell you it's fun, it's engaging, and it's interesting—it's a game.

3 With even shorter pushes from my seat, Picasso has shortened his stride into a medium walk; his right hind is stepping in the footprint of his right fore. As you can see from the background, I ask him to maintain this shorter stride for only a few steps before I ...

4 ... lengthen my pushes to ask for longer strides again. (In response, his right hind is stepping in front of his right-fore footprint again.) Picasso's head has come up a little but I ignore it; at this point, that's just not an issue.

5 What happens when Picasso doesn't shorten stride in response to shorter pushes from my seat? I remind him what I want by reinforcing my seat with the reins, but I don't make a big deal out of it. I simply sit taller and squeeze my shoulder blades together. My heel, hip, and shoulder stay aligned, I still have a straight line from my elbow to the bit, but I've definitely created a "non-allowing" feel of his mouth. This is a feel I maintain until ...

6 ... he responds (or, in this case, over-responds by nearly coming to a halt). At this, I immediately soften the contact and resume the shorter pushes that ask for shorter strides. My softening release here may be a bit over-exaggerated, but I'm OK with that because I'm telling him loud and clear that by shortening his stride he did the right thing.

Your horse may not immediately understand or respond to your pushes. Don't get mad; and whatever you do, don't punish him. Give him a couple of strides to make sure you're not getting a response; then, if you aren't, just take your lower legs a few inches away from his side and cheerfully but matter-of-factly give him a sharp thump that tells him, "Hey! My seat is saying 'take longer strides.' Make your stride match my seat." (For the greatest effect, try to thump him when the hind leg on that side is just coming off the ground.)

Once he does respond, stop "pushing" and just keep your seat swinging in harmony with his motion. It's now his job to maintain that longer stride until you tell him otherwise. If he makes a mistake and slows or takes shorter steps, go ahead and use longer, stronger pushes again (followed by a thump if necessary) to remind him of his part in the proceedings.

A big, nice, ground-covering walk is a very good thing, so continue on for at least half the length of your arena before you ...

Ask for Shorter Strides

Stretch up your upper body, "grow tall," and shorten your pushes (think of asking the swing not to go so high, of polishing a bit less of the saddle, or of raising the back legs of the stool—but not as far from the floor). If, after a stride or two, your horse continues at the same stride length, smoothly take as much feel of the reins as you need to tell him, "Hey! Come back here. My seat is telling you to shorten your stride." Maintain the contact until he does take a shorter step; then you should reward him by moving your hands forward and softening back to a long or loose contact.

It's very important that you don't dwell on this shorter walk, or try to make it shorter and shorter. Even on a long rein, asking for more than a few steps of it at a time can rob your horse's walk of drive, relaxation, and freedom. Get it, but then after four or five steps use longer pushes that ask him to go more forward with longer strides again. Continue alternating longer and shorter pushes until he immediately responds to your seat with longer and shorter steps.

and Wrongs ...

1 If I try to drive Picasso into taking longer strides by rocking back onto my pockets (and the cantle of the saddle), my upper body collapses, I fall behind the motion, I lose the straight line from heel to hip to shoulder, and the backward-angled seam on the side of my breeches clearly shows that my seat bones have rolled forward where they tell him to "slow down and get hollow."

2 If I try to pull him into taking longer strides by arching my back and perching forward on my crotch, I get ahead of the motion and put more weight on his forehand, which just encourages him to go downhill. Yes, there's a straight line from heel to hip to shoulder, but the seam on the side of my breeches shows that my seat bones have rotated toward the rear of my saddle. If they're giving any push at all (my seat is basically immobile and ineffective in this position), it's a backward push. To make matters worse, my thigh and knee have come off the saddle, I've clamped the back of my lower leg on his side, and my toe is sticking almost straight out. Yuck!

3 This is the wrong way to take a feel of the reins: by leaning back and pulling. I'm waaaay behind Picasso's center of gravity. Instead of using a firmer contact that says "whoa," I'm just pulling on his face; that's making him stick his head up, pin his ears, and hollow his back. Compare his expression here to that in photo 5 on page 11; it's clear that here, instead of being interested in what I'm asking and calm about responding, he's annoyed, resistant, unhappy—and probably clueless about what I want.

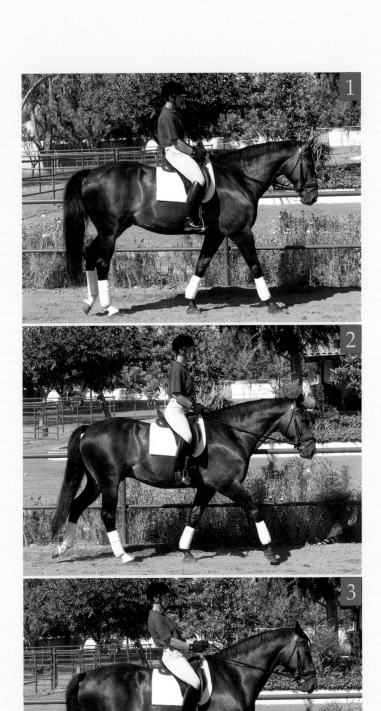

CHAPTER 2

GYMNASTIC EXERCISE 2:
A SHALLOW SERPENTINE

Learn how, by changing your balance, you'll change your horse's bend and direction.

I am guiding Montero through the right bend by sitting deeper on my right seatbone and pushing him to the right with my left leg.

THIS LESSON'S GYMNASTIC—A shallow serpentine with lots and lots of loops—is just as simple as the one in the last chapter… and just as powerful a basic training tool. It builds on increasing the right kind of communication between you and your horse, because you ask with, and he responds to, subtle, almost invisible cues from your seat.

As a reminder, when I say "seat" I mean that part of your body from your seat bone down through your thigh to just below your knee. You learn to push with your seat and leg, rather than pull with your hand.

A beneficial byproduct? You'll once again be teaching your horse to steer by listening to you and balancing himself, instead of leaning on the rail. And because he's not quite certain what you're going to ask him to do next, he'll be more inclined to stay involved and interested in the work.

Here's the Pattern

You'll loop your horse back and forth through the curves of a shallow serpentine (see the diagram on page 14), encouraging him to bend evenly from the tip of his ears to the top of his tail, using little more than a slight increase in the weight on your inside seat bone and some pressure from your outside leg. As you did in Chapter 1, you'll ride the gymnastic at the walk on a

(Continued on page 16)

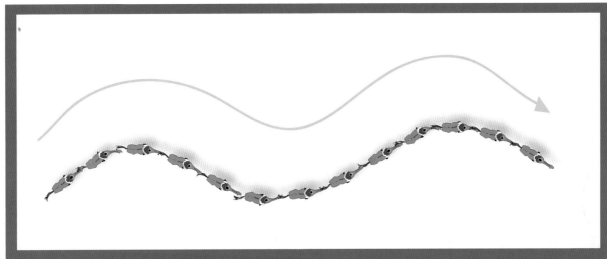

Riding a shallow serpentine, you want to encourage your horse to bend evenly from his ears to his tail with the subtlest of weight and leg aids.

Riding a Serpentine

1 As I start to ask Riitta Saada's Andalusian stallion, Montero, to begin turning to the right, I have a passive "eavesdropping" contact and I'm definitely sitting deeper on my right seat bone, with my weight driven all the way down into my heel. You can't see it, but I'm also rhythmically squeeze-softening/squeeze-softening with my left leg. Additionally, on this first loop of the pattern, I'm showing Montero what I want him to do: An ever-so-slight flexion of my right wrist gently guides his nose to the right. And he's responding with a nice bend through his body, from the tip of his ears to the top of his tail.

2 As we approach the imaginary centerline down the middle of the serpentine, I turn off the rhythmical pressure of my outside (left) leg, bring it forward to the girth, and even up the weight in my seat bones. This tells Montero that I now want him "in neutral," with a straight spine and an even balance between my reins and legs. We'll stay this way for a few more strides, so he's completely balanced and relaxed ...

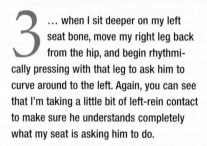

3 ... when I sit deeper on my left seat bone, move my right leg back from the hip, and begin rhythmically pressing with that leg to ask him to curve around to the left. Again, you can see that I'm taking a little bit of left-rein contact to make sure he understands completely what my seat is asking him to do.

4 And he responds very well indeed. He's relaxed, and—all on his own—he's bending and stretching his outside (right) shoulder and foreleg around and away from my leg pressure. This time I don't have to use any inside rein to help him; he's responding completely to my outside leg and my balance on the inside. Note, by the way, that even though my weight and balance have shifted, my upper body has remained upright, with my shoulders level and square.

5 As we complete the shallow left turn and once again approach the "neutral" zone, I'm still on my inside seat bone, but I've relaxed the pressure from my outside leg.

6 This time, as I shift my weight to the new (right) inside seat bone, Montero's head comes up and he stiffens a bit. I don't panic and start fussing with his mouth. Instead I take a very slight, very gentle inside-rein contact, stay deep on the right, press him around with my left leg, and allow the pattern ...

7 ... to relax and soften him right back down again as he takes the new bend and begins another shallow loop to the right. As he relaxes I return to my rhythmic squeeze-softening with my left leg.

loose or passive rein contact so you're free to focus 100 percent on your timing, the coordination you need to switch smoothly from one inside seat bone and outside leg to the other, and your horse's balance as he goes from one softly curving loop to the other. (Besides, when you ride off your hand you tend to shut down your seat, which invariably gets you into a pulling match that he's bound to win!)

Ready? Read "Change the Bend by Degree" on page 18. Then let's get right on with …

How to Ride the Pattern

Pick up an energetic, forward, marching walk. Never forget that a good-quality gait is the most important element of any exercise. (I never ask, "What's wrong with the quality of my canter pirouette?" I ask, "What's wrong with the quality of my canter?") Sit tall with depth in your heels, your shoulders and hips perpendicular across the track you're on, and your weight evenly distributed on both seat bones. Even though you're on a loose or passive contact, make sure you have the classic

straight line from your elbow to your hand to your horse's bit.

Find the centerline of your arena or the middle of a field. If you happen to be out hacking, go to the middle of the trail. (As you can see in the photos on pages 14–15, I'm using a driveway next to my dressage arena.) Ask your horse to start the serpentine by making a shallow loop to the right. Use your eye to pick out a focal point and mentally draw a line to where you're going—but don't do that by cranking your head so far around that he asks, "What is she looking at?" Just keep your chin up, use peripheral vision to locate yourself and the pattern in your work space, and glance ahead at your next objective. In this case, that's a spot a few meters beyond centerline, or the edge of the trail.

Keep your shoulders square and level as you smoothly shift and sit a bit deeper on the inside right. Drop your weight all the way down through your seat bone, your thigh, your lower leg at the girth, and into your heel, which is right beneath your hip and shoulder. This shift in weight and balance is not a big move that's

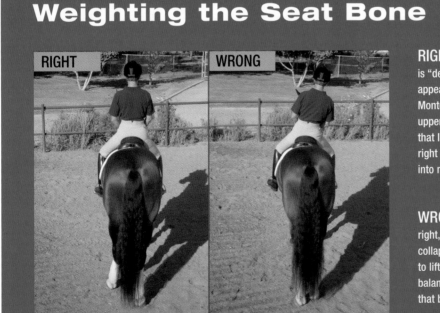

Weighting the Seat Bone

RIGHT

WRONG

RIGHT: How deep on your right seat bone is "deep"? No more than this. Even though I appear absolutely dead straight sitting on Montero, with my shoulders square and my upper body erect, look closely and you'll see that I definitely have more weight from my right seat bone down through my thigh and into my heel.

WRONG: By tipping waaay over to the right, I'm dropping my right shoulder and collapsing my right side, which almost serves to lift my right hip and drives my weight and balance toward the left. How confusing can that be for Montero?

obvious to anyone who's watching. It's not, as I've sometimes seen riders do, practically standing up in your stirrups, swinging your hips over to the right, then plopping back down again. And it's not tilting your upper body right as if you're riding around a curve on a twisty mountain road. Instead it's more as if you're sitting on a

> **Your horse should respond by looking and bending evenly around to the right, from the tip of his ears to the top of his tail.**

surfboard in the ocean and you want to adjust for a swell or to change direction slightly; anything more than a tiny shift of balance on your part and you'll end up in the water. (Your horse certainly doesn't need a more obvious aid. Remember, if he can feel a fly on his side … .)

At the same time you shift your weight and balance, bring your outside left leg slightly back from the hip to where it's a bit behind the girth. Encourage him to follow your shift and curve around to the right by pressing and softening your left leg in time with his walk rhythm. Don't clamp your leg on and just squeeze; like the constant pressure of his girth, that's a pressure he'll tune out because it's always there. Instead, use your leg like a telegraph operator doing Morse Code: When he holds down the button continuously, there's just one long, humongous beep; what message is that? When he doesn't put the button down at all, there's complete silence—and what message is that? But when he taps the button up and down, holding the contact slightly longer at some times than at other times, but always within a rhythm, that's when you get the "dot, dot, dash, dot, dash" message that says something.

Your horse should respond by looking and bending evenly around to the right, from the tip of his ears to the top of his tail. If he just keeps walking straight, help him understand with your inside rein (and, if necessary, a "thump" of your outside leg). Keep your right hand close to his withers (his center of gravity), squeeze your fingers on the rein, and flex or rotate your wrist just enough to

How Not to Turn a Horse

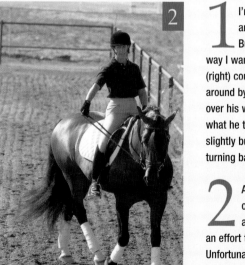

1 I'm sitting on my right inside seat bone and pressing with my outside left leg. But instead of showing Montero the way I want him to go with a slight inside (right) contact, I'm trying to neck-rein him around by raising my left hand and crossing it over his withers. And he's obediently doing what he thinks I'm telling him to do: very slightly bulging his right shoulder and almost turning back to the left.

2 Again, my seat and leg aids are correct, but I've straightened my right arm and taken my right hand wide in an effort to pull him into a right turn. Unfortunately, all I'm doing is pulling his nose and neck so far to the right that his left shoulder is bulging out—yet allowing him to continue toward where he was going.

point your knuckles toward your outside (left) hip. Now hold this slight inside-rein contact until he starts to turn and bend to the right; then immediately soften and return to your loose or passive contact. Yes, you may have to help him understand while he's learning, but your goal is to do this pattern with as little rein as possible. You want him to learn that when you change your balance through your seat bone, he changes the bend through his body.

OK! You've looped around to the right, and now you're ready to loop back to the left, right?

Wrong! The easiest way to unbalance and upset your horse is to ask him to go from one bend to the other without first allowing him to get straight for several strides, which is what I consider the equestrian

> Learning now to relieve the pressure, quietly change position, then reapply pressure will pay off big-time later on, when you want to go smoothly and quickly from shoulder-in to haunches-in, say, or to do flying changes.

equivalent of shifting through "neutral" in a car. (Interestingly enough, the only time you need "neutral" on a horse is when you change from one bend to the other. At all other times—and not just when you're circling or turning, but even on the rail, the centerline, or

the diagonal—you sit a little bit deeper on the inside seat bone.)

So first soften the pressure of your outside (left) leg; then bring it forward to the girth. (Learning now to relieve the pressure, quietly change position, then reapply pressure will pay off big-time later on, when you want to go smoothly and quickly from shoulder-in to haunches-in, say, or to do flying changes.) Equalize the balance and weight in your seat bones. And remember this is not a big, obvious move. It's more like shifting a glass of milk from your right hand to your left. You don't toss or drop the glass, and there's always a moment in the handover from right to left when both hands are holding the glass, no matter how briefly.

Once you're sitting evenly in the middle of your horse and he feels straight (as if he's centered between your hands and legs on a 4-inch balance beam, so there's nowhere else to go to either side) ask him to bend and turn to the left. Shift a penny's worth of weight to your left seat bone, bring your new outside (right) leg back from your hip, and rhythmically start pressing him around so your shallow loop flows freely forward. Continue the serpentine—ending and curving right, straightening and going through neutral, bending and curving left—for as many loops as you can fit in. You can change directions and repeat. Then you'll be ready for our next chapter: Softening your horse's jaw.

Change the Bend by Degree

I like to think of my balance as being like a couple of piles of pennies. When my horse and I are "in neutral" and tracking straight, I have ten pennies in each seat bone. To ask him to begin the shallow serpentine by bending and turning, I take one penny from my left seat bone and move it over to my right seat bone, so I now have nine and eleven. To bend and turn back to the left, I first take the eleventh penny from my right seat bone to my left, so my seat bones, balance, and weight are even; only after that do I transfer another penny from my

right seat bone so I have nine on the right and eleven on the left, where I'm a penny's worth "deeper" and heavier.

As I bring a horse further along in his training, of course, I can shift more pennies faster—the canter zigzag, for example, can involve the exchange of five pennies in the blink of an eye. But even then, there's always a split "neutral" second when I'm ten and ten and everything's even. And whether I'm shifting one penny at a time or ten, nobody sees it—but I know it, and my horse feels it.

CHAPTER 3

GYMNASTIC EXERCISE 3:
SOFTEN YOUR HORSE'S JAW

Start controlling his bend ...

and the balance in his shoulders.

Cassiano is quietly standing still while I flex his jaw to the right with an indirect right rein.

B Y NOW, EVEN IF YOU'VE SPENT ONLY A little time doing my first two gymnastics, your horse should be willingly going forward, coming back, and bending and straightening in response to little more than your seat, weight, and balance. I've had you doing these lessons on a long or loose contact so both of you can focus on just those aids. Now it's time to add some refinement. In this chapter you'll teach your horse to yield to the pressure of your inside rein so he:

- **Lowers his poll.**
- **Softens in the jowl area** (the crease where his head joins his neck).
- **Relaxes his jaw.**
- **And stretches forward and down.**

The result? He creates a little less bit contact on the inside and a little more on the outside. This means he can't brace against the bit as he can when he's perfectly straight, which makes you less likely to pull on his mouth. Although I don't often like to say "always" around horses, when you flex your horse to the inside right, he always balances onto his outside left shoulder. When you flex him to the inside left, he always balances onto his outside right shoulder.

And whatever movement, figure, or pattern you do in dressage, the outside shoulder is where his balance needs to be. (Note, however, that I'm talking about softening and flexing his jaw and jowl; I'm NOT talking about bending his neck. When you bend his neck to the right, he's not so much balanced on the left as leaning or bulging, which we don't want.)

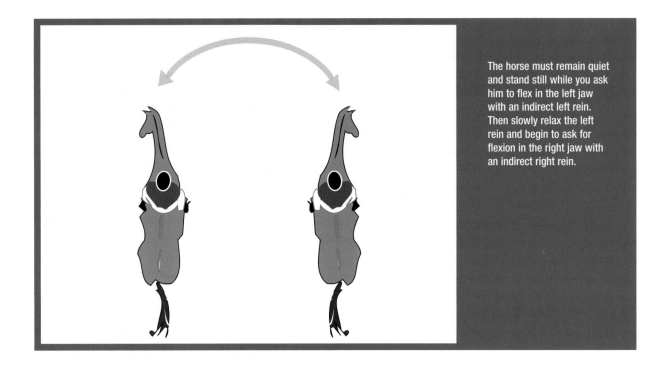

The horse must remain quiet and stand still while you ask him to flex in the left jaw with an indirect left rein. Then slowly relax the left rein and begin to ask for flexion in the right jaw with an indirect right rein.

When you learn to soften your horse's jaw whatever his sport, and whether he's young, green, or simply "uneducated," everything else you do with him will become easier, more correct, and more productive with this training tool. He'll be even more supple and responsive when he's bending, steering, and turning. And the relaxation over his topline that results will allow and encourage him to step forward from behind with increased energy and reach.

Here's What You'll Do

I'm actually going to start off by telling you what you won't do—which is get on your horse. About the worst place to start teaching him to flex and soften his jaw is from his back. Why? Because you, his rider, tend to complicate and confuse matters with your weight and with distracting attempts to stop, start, turn, and steer. That's why you'll do the first part of this exercise standing on the ground, in front of him, with your thumbs hooked through the bit rings. Not only is this method safe and sane, it gives both of you a chance to isolate and understand this one individual aid under very quiet, controlled circumstances. Once he's got the idea and you've got the feel, you'll try it from his back, first at the halt and later at the walk, trot, and canter.

How handy, basic, and useful a training tool is this? I teach it to green babies and to new horses I'm about to ride—no matter what level of "training" I'm told they have. I even use it to run a quick daily check and reminder on my Grand Prix horse, Harmony's Cassiano (this chapter's model).

Soften His Jaw From the Ground

Tack up and get ready to ride. Then back your horse into a corner of his stall, the wash rack, or some other enclosed but familiar place where he can't back up but won't feel trapped. Put the reins over his neck and stand directly in front of him. Assume a balanced, secure, but relaxed position, with your knees a little bent, one foot slightly forward, and one foot slightly back. If he pushes or shoves, this solid stance will be your best defense against getting tossed. Stand quietly for a moment and take a deep breath to center yourself and settle.

Softly establish a light, passive contact with your horse's mouth by hooking your right thumb through the left—his left—bit ring and your left thumb through his right ring. Lightly fold the fingers of both hands around their respective reins, and rest both thumbs on their respective index fingers. Making sure your horse's head and neck are coming straight toward you, start asking him to yield and soften his jaw to the right: Apply an indirect "inside right rein" by pressing your left thumb steadily and gradually on the bit ring until the bit moves about half an inch in a diagonal direction toward his opposite left shoulder. Keep the pressure firm but flexible.

As you press, watch and feel for your horse to do one or more of the following: lower his poll, relax his jowl and his jaw, stretch his nose forward and down, allow the under-muscles of his neck to soften. As soon as he shows you any of these reactions, no matter how slight, immediately relax your left hand to a passive contact—the clearest reward you can give him. You're nowhere near your eventual goal of a fluid, feather-light,

instantaneous give, but you've gotten a positive reaction, and that's terrific.

More than likely, though, his first reaction will be to brace his jaw, root, or try to raise his head. Just keep the solid, steady, lively pressure, but start adding pressure from your right thumb, making the "outside left rein" massage, or ever-so-slightly slide, the bit in his mouth.

This is important: Everything you're doing here on the ground, you're going to repeat from the saddle, which is why I'm referring to "inside" and "outside." This massaging action on the outside rein will eventually become your half-halt. And because the rhythm and timing of your half-halts relate directly to

Soften His Jaw From the Ground

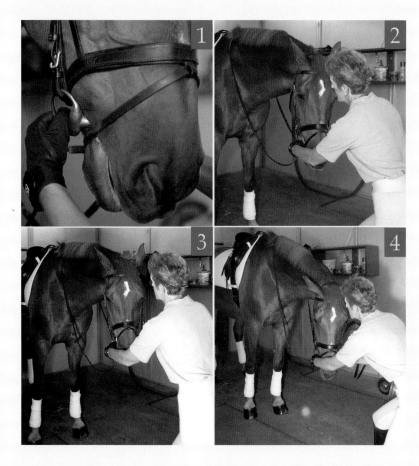

1 Standing in front of Cassiano in the wash rack, I hook my thumbs through the bit rings and ask him to soften and flex to the right by ever-so-slightly rotating my left knuckles toward his left shoulder.

2 This is how you want your horse to look: very calm, with his eye soft (Cassiano almost looks half asleep), the under-muscles of his neck relaxed, and a nice "rainbow" of muscles starting to emerge along his topline. (For stability, and to be able to drop down with him as he stretches, I'm standing with my right foot forward, my left foot back, and knees a little bent.)

3 Cassiano flexes even more to the right (but no further than the point of his shoulder) and you can see that he's still only flexing in his jowl. His neck is still coming very straight out of his shoulders; his perfectly level ears tell you he's not tilting his head to evade the softening.

4 This is a really gooooood stretch. Cassiano's nose doesn't need to touch the ground to tell me he's softly flexed right. He's not tipping his head, his jaw is relaxed, and he's nicely stretched over his topline. At this point, I can soften my contact, allow him to straighten, tell him he's a good boy, then ask him to flex back the other way.

the rhythm and tempo of your horse's gaits, resist the temptation to flutter, jiggle, vibrate, or rattle the bit. Imagine, instead, that he is walking or trotting rhythmically, and lightly massage the bit in time to that gait. Keep the steady pressure on the inside rein. Above all, do not seesaw. Repeatedly dropping the pressure on one side and taking it on the other teaches him nothing. It may seem as if he will never stop leaning, but in fact, he will probably take no more than a few seconds to relax his resistance, drop his nose forward, soften, and create a slight hollow in his right jowl. Again, that's enough for now.

Even if he's the softest, most compliant, most flexible creature in the world, never flex him so his nose goes past the point of his shoulder. To flex beyond that point, he'll have to start bending his neck. Not only will this unbalance him; because his hip can't bend that much, it will make a correct bend through his body from poll to tail impossible.

Problem-solving? If your horse manages to take a step back, instantly relax the pressure, quietly walk him forward, and start again. If he drops behind the vertical or gets a kink or twist in his neck, relax the pressure, bring both your hands toward your chest to straighten

Soften His Jaw Under Saddle

1 I started with Cassiano standing straight, on a long rein. Then I gathered up the reins and asked him to flex to the right by putting a few pennies' worth more weight on my right seat bone and rotating my right wrist to turn my knuckles toward my left hip. This is as much flexion as I'd want: His neck is still coming very straight out of his shoulder and his nose is just about where it should be—in line with his shoulder. If I were going to be picky about something, I'd say my upper body should be more upright, and I shouldn't be dropping my right shoulder and tipping my head to LOOK for the flexion. And Cassiano's poll is not the ideal highest point, although that doesn't bother me so much—he's within an acceptable range where he's calmly softening and flexing.

2 I allow him to start lessening his flexion to the right by relaxing the pressure of my right rein (still maintaining contact), and starting—a penny at a time—to even the weight on my seat bones.

3 Now sitting pretty much equal on my two seat bones, I have a very even contact on both reins, and in the next moment Cassiano will be dead straight (what I described in Chapter 2 as "in neutral.") Then I can ask him to …

him, and start again. If he flips his nose and knocks you off balance, relax the pressure and get reorganized. And no matter what he does, don't punish him. Just calmly and cheerfully persist until he realizes that yielding to rein pressure is as OK as it is inevitable. Once he's softened to right and left, you're ready to …

Soften His Jaw Under Saddle

First loosen up by doing some forward and back and a few shallow serpentines on a long or loose rein with a passive contact. (See Chapters 1 and 2 to refresh your memories on these exercises, if needed.) Then halt as

square and balanced as you can without fussing at your horse. Make sure your seat tells him to stand still: Sit quietly, and let your leg rest lightly on his side. If he steps back, by all means, push with your seat and squeeze with your legs to move him forward a couple of steps. But remember, you've spent the last two chapters teaching him to respond in an energetically forward way to your seat and legs—now you can use their "absence" to tell him to stand still.

With your torso upright and stretched tall, elbows at your sides, and hands close to and low over the withers, ask your horse to soften his jaw to the right.

4 … start flexing left by slightly shifting my weight to my left seatbone and rotating my inside left wrist so my left knuckles start to turn toward my right hip. As I ask for …

5 … a bit more flexion, notice that his neck is still coming straight out of his shoulders, he's calm and relaxed—and I'm happy to say that my upper body is much more upright and square.

6 Cassiano's nose is just over the point of his left shoulder: that's as far as I want him to flex. I'll smoothly straighten him again by relaxing my inside rein and evening my seat bones. Now go back and study the photos with an eye toward the balance in Cassiano's shoulders. When I'm sitting on my right seat bone and he's flexed right, he's ever so slightly balanced on his left shoulder. When I'm sitting evenly on both seat bones and he's almost straight, his balance is pretty much even between his shoulders. And when I'm sitting on my left seat bone and he's flexed left, he's balanced on his right shoulder. That kind of balance is your ultimate goal.

First put a little more weight on your inside (right) seat bone, just as you did in Chapter 2 to ask him to turn and bend right on the shallow serpentine. (How powerful will this aid eventually be for you? To this day, when I sit on my long-retired Grand Prix partner Hannabal and I put a feather's more weight on my right seat bone, he automatically flexes his jaw to the right and vice versa.

> You've spent the last two chapters teaching him to respond in an energetically forward way to your seat and legs—now you can use their "absence" to tell him to stand still.

Take a light, "sponge-squeezing" feel on the inside rein as you softly turn your right knuckles toward your left hip. If your horse softens, relaxes his jaw, stretches his nose forward and down, drops his poll, and creates that slight hollow in his right jowl—even the littlest bit—that's great. And guess what? He will have created his own reward: a release from contact. He will also be demonstrating the first signs of what will eventually become self-carriage. Stop taking. Just keep your hand still, scratch his neck, and tell him what a really good boy he is!

If he bores down, sticks his nose in the air, rolls his neck up, comes behind the vertical, or twists his neck, just stay tall and ask more clearly for his right jaw to soften by rotating your right knuckles even more toward your left hip at the same time you start slowly and rhythmically massaging and sliding the bit on the left (outside) rein. When he softens, remember to tell him he's good. Pause; then soften, allow him to straighten—never go from one bend to the other without straightening first—and ask him to flex to the left (remember to change the weight in your seat).

Tips for Good Training

■ **Be prepared.** Use a plain snaffle with a loose ring or an eggbutt, a cavesson that's loose enough for two or three fingers' room, and, if you think you need it to remind your horse to keep his mouth quiet and closed around the bit, a flash (again, loose enough for two or three fingers).

■ **Be careful.** A few horses feel trapped and panicky the first time they experience this kind of pressure. If your horse starts looking wild-eyed, tries to rear, or hollows out and sticks his head in the air, immediately release all pressure, pat him, and tell him, "This is really OK." Try again, but if he's really upset, go and do something else altogether. Then check with your vet to make sure you're not dealing with a physical problem that needs attention. If your vet clears him and he's still upset, try consulting a qualified professional who may be able to smooth the way for both of you.

■ **Be patient.** If your horse softens fine on the ground but argues, backs up, and acts confused under saddle, soften him on the ground for a few more weeks. Or ask your trainer or a knowledgeable friend to stand in front of your horse with you in the saddle and remind him what you're looking for. Once he makes the connection, your helper can back off and you can take over from the saddle again.

■ **Be smart.** Flex any horse before you get on to make sure he knows how to yield to the rein. Yes, you can grab your bucking strap in a sudden bolting or spinning emergency—but when you know the horse will yield to pressure on the rein, you also have a control button you can push.

■ **Fine-tune your feel.** How should your contact feel? I like to think of it as holding a baby's hand as he's taking his first steps: You don't let go so he falls, but you don't crush his fingers or pull his arm out of its socket either. If he starts to lose his balance, you take a slightly firmer feel to give him a steadier support; once he's on his feet, you lighten again.

■ **Graduate to gaits.** Once your horse is softening his jaw at the halt under saddle, try it at the walk, trot, and finally, the canter. Just remember that as soon as you're in motion, the influence equation changes considerably: from 100 percent hand and rein aids creating the yielding to about 85 percent seat and leg aids creating forward energy and 15 percent hand and rein aids creating yielding.

■ **Be consistent.** Repeat this pattern once or twice every day—but no more—always working toward using less pressure than the day before to get more response. It may take weeks or even months, but with time, you'll touch the bit and he'll drop and lower and bend in any direction you want, and to almost any degree.

WRONG Ways To Soften His Jaw

1 Not only is my back hunched; I'm trying to get Cassiano to flex by crossing my inside hand over his withers. My wrist is straight, my arm rigid and stiff from elbow to knuckles, I'm sticking my elbow out, I'm raising my inside hand, and I've completely lost the straight line from elbow to bit. Worst of all, I'm causing Cassiano to bend his neck at the shoulder. He's not evenly bent from poll to tail, and overbending his neck makes him bulge or lean into his outside shoulder instead of balancing on it. (He is flexing somewhat, because he's a schooled horse.)

2 This time, instead of crossing my inside hand over the withers, I'm trying to pull Cassiano into a flexion with an inside leading rein that has waaay over-bent his neck and taken his nose well beyond the point of his shoulder. Again, I've totally lost the straight line from elbow to hand to bit.

3 Although I'm pretty much sitting in a correct position, with weight in my left seat bone and my upper body fairly erect, I'm asking for way too much flexion, which finally makes Cassiano …

4 … curl up, come behind the vertical, put his chin on his chest, and flex at the fifth vertebra instead of at the poll—an evasion that, once a horse learns it, can be impossible to un-teach him.

CHAPTER 4

GYMNASTIC EXERCISE 4:
HALF-HALTS DEMYSTIFIED

Use this simple exercise to enhance and refine communication with your horse and improve his way of going.

Whatever a horse's ability or sport, a half-halt will help him move the best he possibly can. He will have more suspension or "air time," looking almost as if he's traveling on his tiptoes, as Cassiano does here.

FOR THE FIRST TWO GYMNASTIC exercises in this book, "forward and back" and the shallow serpentine, I purposely had you keep a long, loose, or passive contact on the reins. You could focus on specific cues from your all-important seat, weight, and balance, and your horse could learn to respond to them. In Chapter 3 you took up a contact and taught him to yield to the pressure of a direct rein by lowering his poll, flexing his jowl, relaxing his jaw, and stretching his nose forward and down. This not only started making him more supple and responsive about bending, steering, and turning, but it set the stage (as you'll see) for this lesson: half-halts.

What IS a Half-Halt?

Simply speaking, it's an outside rein aid, made by squeezing your outside shoulder back to create a slightly stronger pressure or feel on the bit. This pressure raises your horse's outside shoulder and makes his outside fore pause momentarily in its forward flight. And this pause,

in combo with a squeeze and push of your seat and leg, encourages his inside hind to step farther and more powerfully underneath and engage.

Now, before we say any more, there is a critical point that I want to clarify. You read in lots of dressage "how-to" books that you've got to get your horse's engine going so you can drive his hind end up to his front end; you never want to ride "front to back." That's absolutely true. But if your horse is on his forehand, as most horses naturally are, and you don't do something to elevate his shoulders enough to make room for his hind legs to step underneath himself, you can kick, kick, kick,

Feel the Half-Halt Yourself

1 Here's a great way to practice the feel of a half-halt at a standstill on your horse but without disturbing him. As I sit, quiet and relaxed but correct in my position, my assistant Bettina stands in front of Cassiano's chest and takes hold of the reins on both sides of his neck. She establishes a good contact between her hands and mine, with a slight slack between her hands and the bit. Now I can "practice" half-halts to totally get the feel of them from the saddle—but because they'll stop at her hands, they won't affect his mouth.

2 And here's my half-halt: I squeeze my left shoulder back and down. This simple motion raises my chest and flattens my back. It "sucks" me down into the saddle, so my seat and legs can communicate more effectively with my horse. It slightly pushes my inside (right) seat bone more forward and down, which enhances the effect of inside leg to outside rein. And it automatically brings my left elbow and hand slightly back (compare this photo with the previous one), which creates a stronger contact on Bettina's right hand without any muscling, pulling, or jerking by my hand and arm—which have stayed quite relaxed.

and drive and push, but you'll just make him more on his forehand and more strung out. His haunches will actually start pushing out behind his body.

A half-halt will help a horse move the best he possibly can. He'll have more suspension. (When my Grand Prix horse Cassiano, our demo horse in this chapter, does a passage—a very collected, very elevated, and very cadenced trot—his front feet hardly touch the ground.) And it only gets better: The more your horse responds to your half-halts in that way, the stronger he'll grow and so sustain this new way of going, which is what we call "self-carriage."

What's more, depending on when, where, and how you give it, a half-halt:

■ Asks your horse for an upward or downward transition (and that can be within a gait, where you go from a working trot to a lengthened trot, for example, or between gaits, such as going from canter to trot).

■ Gives a "wake-up call" that something is going to change and he's about to do something different. That could be, say, come off the rail and circle at B, change bend and direction on a shallow serpentine, go from tracking straight to a half-pass.

■ Reminds him that he's always supposed to match the tempo and rhythm in your seat, whether he needs that reminder because you're trotting along at a nice, energetic pace and he suddenly fizzles and dies under you, or because he picks up speed and starts rolling along.

Before diving into the mechanics of how to ride a half-halt and the aids you'll need to use, I want to go over a few prerequisites for making it work.

What a Half-Halt Needs

■ **Inside flexion.** As I showed you in Chapter 3, inside flexion balances your horse a bit more onto his outside shoulder. It also lets you half-halt against the flexion, which allows the effect of the half-halting rein aid to move all the way up and over his poll and neck to his shoulder. If he isn't flexed when you try to half-halt, you

> As with any aid, you have to hold a half-halt long enough to get that waiting, hovering response from your horse.

just jerk or pull on the outside corner of his mouth; in response, he braces, curls up and comes behind the vertical, throws his nose in the air, or turns his nose to the outside. The half-halt dies right there.

■ **Timing.** As I told you when you started the "forward

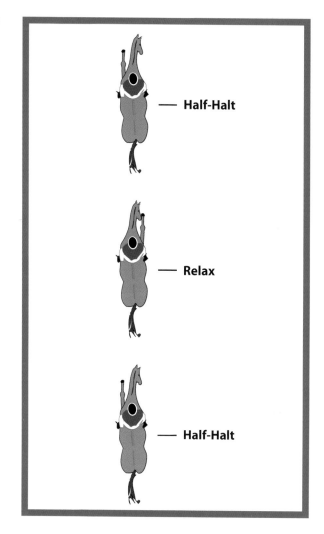

— Half-Halt

— Relax

— Half-Halt

and back" gymnastic in Chapter 1, timing simply means giving an aid or correction when it's going to have a positive effect. By and large, that's during what I call the up-beat: the moment when the foot or feet you want to influence are coming up off the ground and beginning their forward flight. The worst—or least effective—time, and the one most likely to send mixed messages and cause confusion and frustration, is the down-beat, when the foot or feet you want to affect are heading toward or arriving on the ground.

You want to influence your horse's outside shoulder, so look for the moment when his outside fore is coming off the ground. That moment is fairly clear in the four-beat walk (refresh your memory about the several ways to detect his walking footfalls by reviewing Chapter 1's

A Half-Halting Stride at the Trot

1 As we complete the "sit" phase of the posting trot, Cassiano is nicely energetic (a key to a successful half-halt) and flexed to the inside. I'm relaxed but correct in the saddle with a normal contact on the outside rein.

2 In the next moment, as Cassiano puts his inside fore down and begins to bring his outside fore off the ground, I start to rise out of the saddle and begin my half-halt by squeezing my outside shoulder back and down. Nothing else changes. My riding position is still correct and pure, with my shoulder over my hip and my hip over my deep heel.

3 At the highest point of my post, and the "peak" of my half-halt, my outside shoulder is well back. Without jerking, pulling, or making a big, obvious correction, I've "paused" Cassiano's outside left shoulder in its forward flight and raised his chest. Now, with a forward thrust of my hip and a "bear hug" down through my thigh into my upper calf, I can encourage him to step more forward and engage from behind.

"Forward and Back"). It's a very clear moment to feel in the three-beat canter. And it's a piece of cake at the two-beat posting trot, because it's the moment when you're rising out of the saddle.

■ **Rhythm.** I see lots of riders, especially in the hunter ranks, give a half-halt as a quick, sharp jerk. Even if their timing is right, their horses almost NEVER respond or change (except, perhaps, to throw their heads in the air in protest). As with any aid, you have to hold a half-halt long enough to get that waiting, hovering response from your horse. But you also have to soften the hold (relax your outside shoulder and rein) before the down-beat. Otherwise, as I explained above, your half-halt will no longer be effective. What's more, if you don't have that moment of softening or release, you won't be ready to squeeze your outside shoulder back and half-halt again on

the next up-beat. If you hold, hold, hold—well, that's just hanging. And what kind of aid or communication is that?

■ **Position.** You must maintain balance and strength in your core and a pure, effective posture—with a straight, upright torso, good contact from your seat down to just below your knee, and depth in your heels. If you desert any part of that, you're just pulling on the reins, leaning back, or tipping forward. Remember, your horse's posture is nothing more or less than a reflection of yours. If you ride tipped forward, with rounded shoulders, how can he open his chest and bring his shoulders back and up?

With those points in place, let me talk you through …

How to do a Half-Halt

Want to try a half-halt while you're reading this book in

(Continued on page 34)

4 In the next moment, with his inside hind and outside fore starting their descent toward the ground, I relax my outside (half-halting) shoulder so his outside fore can reach very expressively forward and his inside hind can just as expressively engage.

5 As we complete the trot stride, Cassiano is totally engaged on the inside hind and stretching forward on the outside fore, with tons of airtime and suspension. He's nicely bent through the corner from poll to tail, his chest is looking right where he's going, he's maintaining an inside (right) flexion, and you can really see him coming up off the ground. Me? I'm completely relaxed in shoulder and seat, just starting to come back into the saddle and sit again. Without this moment of relaxation, we would not be set up for the next half-halt.

A Half-Halting Stride at the Canter

1 I'm deep in my heel, my elbow is by my side, and what appears to be a slight collapse in my upper body is a naturally flexed response to Cassiano's motion at this moment of the stride. (You have to move your body quite a bit to look as if you're sitting perfectly still on a cantering horse.) His inside fore is still on the ground, and his outside shoulder is still down, but his outside fore is just beginning to lift, so I squeeze my outside shoulder back.

2 That squeeze creates more pressure on the outside rein, pushes my inside seat bone more forward, and lowers me deep into the saddle, where I can most effectively push my seat and inside leg into him. (I wish my inside heel weren't coming up so much.) As his outside fore begins to hover, I can create the energy that encourages his inside hind to step under and engage.

3 Look at the incredible lifting response in Cassiano's shoulder! Now I can really relax my shoulder, soften the pressure on the rein, and drive with my seat and leg (there's that heel again) to get him really reaching up underneath with his inside hind. Again, the apparent collapse in my upper body is just an awkward moment as I'm following Cassiano's stride. In person or on a video, you wouldn't even notice it.

WRONG

4 Ahhh. I totally relax my body from shoulder to heel, and look at how balanced Cassiano is! His inside hind leg is reaching so far forward as it engages that it's practically underneath me.

5 Here's an outside view of the canter half-halt: My outside leg, slightly back from my hip to my heel, is my cue to Cassiano that we're cantering and he's to keep cantering until he hears otherwise from me. My whip in my outside hand is ready if I need to energize his outside hind (always the first step in every canter stride). He's nicely flexed to the inside, and—in response to my half-halt on the outside rein—he's really lifting his shoulders. As a result, he can now respond to the push in my seat by stepping forward more energetically and expressively with his inside hind.

6 WRONG! Here's a great example of the wrong way to half-halt: by riding from front to back. My hand and arm are pointing straight down and pulling so far back that my hand is actually on my thigh. I've completely lost the straight line from elbow to bit—and if I'm trying to squeeze my outside shoulder, it's having no effect at all. I'm not only being ineffective; I'm producing negative results: Cassiano is almost starting to look to the outside because he's losing the flexion to the right.

The bit is very clearly getting pulled through his mouth instead of being allowed to apply light pressure to the corner. And if you compare this photo with any of the others in this chapter, you'll see that his chest is leaning forward and down instead of coming back and up—and, for the first and only time, that his inside right hind is not stepping forward and engaging under his body.

your kitchen or on your tack trunk? As you're sitting there, imagine you're riding your horse and tracking right. Grow tall through your upper body, let your elbows drop down by your sides, bring your hands together as you would when riding, and be sure to close your fingers firmly on your imaginary reins.

First flex your horse's jowl to the inside by rotating your right knuckles toward your left hip. Then, without arching or stiffening your lower back, squeeze your outside left shoulder back and a little down. That's all the motion a half-halt takes, but feel how it slightly pulls your elbow and hand back (and, with it, the rein, to create more pressure on your horse's mouth). Feel how that squeeze in your shoulder makes you sink just a little deeper into the saddle, so your seat can clearly tell him what you want him to do. And feel how it slightly pushes your inside seat bone forward and down for an even more definite "inside leg to outside rein" effect. Then see "A Half-Halting Stride at the Trot" on pages 30–31, for an illustration of how to execute it in the saddle.

Of course, within the half-halt, your seat and legs say "go" and your hands say "whoa"—that basic job description doesn't change. But one aid always has to be

> If your horse is running away with you on the trail, you may need a half-halt that's as "in your face" as a pulley rein.

a bit sooner and stronger than the other, because you can never pull and push at the same time or with equal pressure. For an upward transition, for example, the driving force in your seat, leg, and calf is stronger than the half-halt in your shoulder. For a downward transition, the half-halt is stronger in your upper body—rib cage, stomach, core, and shoulder—than it is in your seat, thigh, and leg.

Another point to remember is that there is no single strength of half-halt. As you experiment, you'll find yourself half-halting on an almost infinite sliding scale. If your horse is running away with you on the trail, you may need a half-halt that's as "in your face" as a pulley rein. Then there's always the chance that you gave a correct, properly timed, normal half-halt to ask him to slow down and match the tempo in your seat, and he just didn't respond. In that case, soften momentarily (remember, you need that moment of relaxation) and, on the next up-beat, "turn up the volume" on your half-halt: not by

jerking or pulling, but by squeezing harder and a hair longer through your shoulder.

If THAT doesn't work, soften again, and on the next up-beat give something closer to a "three-quarter-halt," where you almost bring him down to a walk or halt—but not quite, because you don't want him to walk. You want him to keep trotting; you just want his trot to match your tempo and rhythm. And when he HAS responded, be sure to turn down the volume of your half-halts again.

Tips for Good Training

Finally, when teaching half-halts to my students, I like to remind them of a few more points:

■ **Be whip savvy.** When schooling, carry your whip on the side where it will energize the appropriate hind leg. At the trot, that's usually on the inside, because you want to affect the inside hind. At the canter, it's on the outside, because the first (strike-off) step of every canter stride is with the outside hind.

■ **Half-halt often.** Start incorporating half-halts into everything you're doing, including the patterns you've already worked on. In "forward and back," do an upward transitional half-halt every time you ask your horse to go more forward; give a downward transitional halt-halt to ask him to come back. On the shallow serpentine, each time you go from neutral to a new bend, feel how a half-halt encourages him to lift his outside shoulder and momentarily hover it in the air as he turns around onto the new loop.

■ **Be patient.** Take baby steps. Learning to half-halt and teaching your horse to respond and carry himself won't come overnight. Today you may feel a bit of a response. Tomorrow you may say, "Ooh, he gave me a little bit more." Two weeks later, you may realize that he's not sprawling forward on his forehand any more; in fact, he's coming forward more energetically from behind, with a spring in his step, maintaining a more consistent rhythm and tempo. Be extremely patient in asking for the half-halt and he'll figure it out.

As your horse gets more tuned in to your half-halts, you'll be able to make them as frequent and as subtle as the "lift" in your upper body every time you rise at the posting trot or you take a breath. (Inhale deeply right now and feel how your chest rises and your shoulder comes back just a hair.) These half-halts will be powerful, they'll be effective, nobody watching will be able to see them, but WOW, will the fantastic results be visible for all to see in your horse.

CHAPTER 5

GYMNASTIC EXERCISE 5:
THE NEARLY PERFECT CIRCLE

Use this exercise to get the corner on the most fundamental figure in dressage.

Cones help you ride accurate 20-meter circles. From these, you can create all sorts of figures and movements to help focus your horse's attention and develop his balance, suppleness, and obedience.

OUR HIGH-SCHOOL GEOMETRY books told us that a circle is "a curved line that is everywhere equidistant from a given fixed point, the center." Translation: A circle is perfectly round. It starts and finishes in the same place. A circle is not shaped like an oval, a teardrop, a loop, or a fried egg. At 20 meters in diameter—the full width of a standard dressage arena—it is the first gymnastic figure you ride at Introductory and Training Levels. And as you rise through the dressage levels and your horse becomes stronger, suppler, and more responsive to your aids, the circles you're asked to ride shrink from 15 meters all the way down to 6-meter voltes.

Why does the circle figure so prominently in training our horses?

The Circle is Infinitely Variable ...

... so slice it and dice it, cut it up like a pie, and you can create all sorts of figures and movements. You can attach one full circle to another and make a figure eight. You can use circles to change direction in various ways: Within a circle, you ride two small half-circles in a figure-S shape (called "a change of rein through the circle"); on the rail, you ride a half-circle and return to the track on a diagonal line; or you leave the track on a diagonal line and return to the track by riding a half-circle in reverse. Your first turns up centerline are half 10-meter circles. Each of the four corners in the arena is a quarter-volte. And you make a serpentine by connecting half-circles—anything from two half-circles at 30 meters to three at 20 meters, four at 15 meters, or five at 12 meters. Fold in frequent changes of rein and tempo while you're

Riding the Diamond

1 I'm on an absolutely straight line from the centerline cone at three o'clock to E, or twelve o'clock (see diagram on page 38). Montero's giving me a nice, forward, energetic trot (a prerequisite for any exercise), and he's straight and balanced, with a very slight inside flexion. My weight is in my heels, and my shoulders and hips are absolutely perpendicular to the track. Our eyes are focused on E.

2 Having arrived at E, I'm already looking at nine o'clock and I've already taken just a bit more inside flexion—enough to see Montero's inside eye and make sure he's starting to look there, too. As his outside fore comes off the ground and his outside shoulder starts to come up, I'll half-halt on the outside rein and squeeze with my outside leg to ask him to bring his outside shoulder, leg, and foot around the corner. Note that I'm not pulling on the inside rein to make this turn start to happen; my inside seat and leg are there at the girth to keep the trot coming forward and to make sure he knows he's only supposed to increase the flexion in his jowl, not follow that bend and fall or turn in on the figure.

3 With the turn almost completed, I am NOT half-halting, because Montero's outside fore is on the ground and this is the moment where I'm sitting and I've softened my aids. As soon as his right fore starts to come up (and I start to rise out of the saddle), I will again half-halt on the outside right rein and squeeze or press with my outside right leg to ask him to …

schooling, and these variations focus your horse's attention. They keep him from getting bored or restless. And they develop balance, suppleness (by stretching the muscles on the outside and relaxing those on the inside), and obedience.

To accomplish these goals and to get good scores in your dressage tests—you have to ride every circle accurately (no ovals, fried eggs, or 18-meter circles where the test says 15-meter circles). Your horse has to be "technically" straight, his body evenly bent from poll to tail on the particular curve of the circle you're riding. His hind feet follow exactly in the tracks of his forefeet, his inside hind carries a bit more weight than his outside hind, and he has a little more of his balance on his outside shoulder.

The problem? You can get a little lost—and so lose track of those qualities—trying to ride one big continuously curving line. That's why in this lesson I'm going to show you how to create a nearly perfect 20-meter circle by first riding a diamond: a square with four straight sides and four 90-degree corners (see diagram on page 38). You'll ride the diamond point-to-point (a skill that is critical over fences as well as in the dressage arena), using small traffic cones as visual aids to mark the corners you're aiming for. You'll also apply all the pattern skills you've already started developing: response to your seat, legs, and balance; flexion and bending; and above all, half-halts.

When the diamond feels accurate and comfortable, you'll turn the figure into an octagon—with eight straight

4 ... complete the turn. Montero once again has his weight on his outside fore, I'm in the "sit" phase of the trot, I'm beginning to relax the "turning" inside flexion, and I'm allowing my outside leg to return to a quiet, passive contact.

5 And here we both have our eyes glued to the nine o'clock cone and Montero is dead straight, his chest facing exactly where he's going. He's also very uphill, very engaged, and standing up on his outside shoulder, neither bulging out nor leaning in. As you can see, the steady, quiet repetition of the pattern has instilled a consistency to his frame and attitude, and to my aids.

sides and eight wider corners, again all marked with cones. When that feels smooth and easy and correct, you'll just bow out the octagon's sides a bit and ride each stride as a very subtle form of straight/turn/straight/turn/straight. By then, I promise, you'll have as nearly perfect a circle as can be made. Best of all, you and your horse should easily master this gymnastic in one session.

As you do, you'll start feeling how to do the following:
■ Create an accurate figure with your driving aids, reinforce your horse's response to your half-halts, and improve your control over the balance in his shoulders.
■ Tune up and sharpen the timing of your flexing, half-halting, and turning because with each phase of the pattern you'll have to do them more quickly and more frequently.
■ Use your eyes to ride straight to a specific point. This is a skill that's critical to any pattern or movement, be it a circle, a serpentine, or a half-pass.

■ Develop a system for riding any circle or half-circle, no matter what its size, just by riding to your points.
■ Do a shoulder-in—to ride a corner, your horse has to stretch his outside shoulder up and around. (If I were standing in the middle of your circle, I'd want to see your horse's outside shoulder reaching more forward on the track than his inside shoulder.)
■ Control the shape and size of all the figures I described above and more by controlling each stride your horse takes.

And this brings me to one of my core beliefs: A dressage horse—unlike a jumper or an event horse—is not supposed to think for himself. Yes, he's supposed to be expressive. He should definitely volunteer his energy and intelligence. He should be your partner and enjoy what you're doing together. But getting creative about where or how you ride a figure? Nope. And using crookedness, resistance, or a lazy response to avoid the difficulty of a movement (difficulty that actually builds straightness, suppleness, and strength)? Absolutely not!

Ride the Diamond

Get set up: Place two soccer cones or low markers on the centerline at nine o'clock and three o'clock, as shown on the diagram. (The twelve o'clock and six o'clock corners don't need cones because they're at markers E and B of your dressage arena. If you don't have access to a dressage ring, go ahead and use markers.)

If you'd prefer to ride the pattern at the C end of the arena, set out three cones—two on opposite rails 10 meters from the corner, and one on the centerline 20 meters from C. And if you're a hunter rider (after all, you have to ride nice, straight, balanced lines, too), just set up the pattern anywhere in your arena that lets the circle end up being at least 20 meters in diameter.

Now ride the pattern: Pick up an energetic posting trot, tracking left down the arena rail toward E (twelve o'clock). Stay squarely in the middle of your horse, with your hips and shoulders perpendicular to the track. A stride or two before you arrive at E, start to prepare for the turn: Place a penny's worth more weight on your inside (left) seat

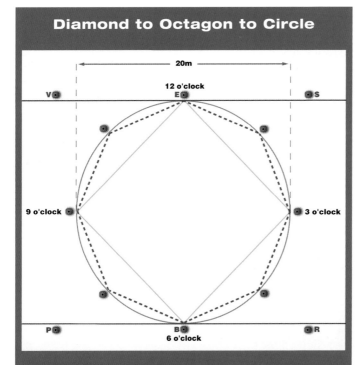

Diamond to Octagon to Circle

20m

12 o'clock
E
9 o'clock
3 o'clock
V   S
P   R
B
6 o'clock

To create a nearly perfect 20-meter circle, you'll first ride a diamond—a square with four straight sides and four 90-degree corners (orange lines). When that feels accurate, you'll turn the figure into an octagon with eight straight sides and eight wider corners (red dotted lines). As that becomes smooth, you'll bow out the octagon's sides to form a circle (green line).

Riding the Octagon

1 Here's a nice corner-turning moment from the front. Instead of using two or three strides to make the turn, we're taking it in one or two. Again, our eyes are already ahead on the next cone and I'm turning Montero with my outside leg and outside half-halting rein, so he's very nicely flexed and balanced. He's evenly bent from poll to tail. And even though his outside fore has just arrived on the ground, you can still see that in flight, his shoulder lifted up and came around—so his chest is very clearly facing where he's going. Because this moment is the down beat, where his weight is on his outside fore, I'm sitting and my aids are relaxed.

2 Now that the corner is finished, Montero is straight in his body and he's trotting straight toward the next cone. Of course, this straightness will only last for another stride or stride and a half before I have to …

3 … ask for more inside flexion, put my outside leg on, and half-halt on my outside rein to ask him to turn the corner again by bringing his outside fore up and around. Both our sets of eyes are already looking ahead toward B.

Wrongs

1 I wish I could say that I'm just asking for waaay too much flexion with my inside rein here, but it's much worse than that—I'm pulling on the inside rein to try to get Montero to follow the circular track. Unfortunately, by overbending him in the neck I'm just letting his outside shoulder bulge out. As a result, his chest and his right fore are actually pointing straight down the rail. He's tilted his head, dropped his inside ear, and flexed at the fifth vertebra instead of the poll so his poll is way too low. And instead of a consistent bend from poll to tail, matching the curving track he's supposed to be on, he's more bent in his neck than in his hip—a real no-no.

Me? With my outside shoulder more forward and higher than my inside shoulder, I'm no longer perpendicular to the track and I'm throwing more weight to the outside.

2 What a mess! Yes, I'm half-halting on the outside rein at the right time—but because I've given up my inside flexing rein, Montero's turning his nose out instead of softening his jaw and momentarily pausing his outside fore. And because I've messed up the balance in his shoulders, he's leaning to the inside instead of standing up on his outside shoulder. Now it's a matter of the chicken and the egg: With him leaning in on his inside shoulder and falling off the circular track, I see that we're not going to get to B and I start trying to pull him there with the outside rein.

bone. Turn your head and look toward the nine o'clock cone on the centerline. Slightly rotate your left knuckles toward your right hip to ask for a little more inside flexion—just enough that you feel your horse soften his jaw and can see his inside eye, telling you he's starting to look toward nine o'clock and balancing himself onto his outside shoulder. But be sure to keep your hips and shoulders perpendicular to the rail so your body language tells him he's still supposed to be going straight.

On the next up beat, as you rise out of the saddle, half-halt on the outside right rein by squeezing your right shoulder back and a little down, so your horse momentarily lifts and pauses his outside shoulder. Then, with your inside (left) leg active enough at the girth to keep the energy and support him so he doesn't fall in while making the figure, squeeze your outside leg (the same way you did in the shallow-loop serpentine in Chapter 2) to ask him to bring his forehand around the corner and onto the straight side of the diamond. This is important: You're not going to ride a geometrically precise 90-degree corner, and you're definitely not going to do any kind of a corner in one stride. Plan on two or three strides to get from straight on the rail to straight on the first side of the diamond. But as you do, try for the feel

and idea of a square corner, with your horse's balance on his outside shoulder, his outside (right) foreleg coming up and around to the inside, his neck coming straight out of his withers, and his shoulders and chest looking where he's going. He should neither "spin" around his middle, lean in and "motorcycle," nor bulge out and keep going straight.

As soon as you've turned the corner and arrived on the straight side, soften the inside flexion just enough to let your horse look straight ahead, maintaining enough flexion that you can still half-halt on the outside rein. (As I explained in Chapter 4, if he isn't a little bit flexed when you half-halt, you end up jerking or pulling on the outside corner of his mouth instead. The effect of the half-halt dies right there and doesn't "go through"—doesn't move all the way up and over his poll and neck to influence his shoulder.) Let your outside (right) leg return to a more passive contact. And sit more squarely in the saddle, your hips and shoulders perpendicular to the track. A stride or two before you arrive at the nine o'clock cone on the centerline, turn your head to look at B and prepare to turn exactly the same way you did at E.

Continue riding the diamond, looking ahead, half-

Tips for Good Training

■ **Look back.** When we started I told you that each exercise builds on the ones that came before. So make sure you have a solid sense of control over what we've already worked on—forward and back, the shallow serpentine, flexing and bending your horse's jaw, and the half-halt. They don't have to be perfect; they're never going to be 100-percent perfect. After all, it's the pursuit of perfection that attracts us to dressage, right?

■ **Post the trot.** Ride this exercise at the posting trot so your horse is nicely forward, you're not distracted by trying to sit the trot and hang on, and you're absolutely clear about the timing of your half-halts. (You give them when his outside fore and inside hind are beginning their flight forward—in other words, when you're rising out of the saddle.)

■ **Adjust the "volume."** Turn the volume up or down on your half-halt according to the shape of your corner. I don't know you or your horse, so I can't give you a precise number on a scale of 1 to 100, or exact pounds of pressure. But for the sharp 90-degree turns on the diamond, use a fairly

unequivocal half-halt to tell him you want him to lift his shoulder and bring it around. For the more open turns on the octagon, tone the half-halt down a bit. And for the circle, where you're riding a straight/turn/straight/turn with every stride, your half-halt will probably be nothing more than a deep inhalation of breath or an extra lift of your chest as you rise out of the saddle. (And once your horse starts understanding, you're going to be able to turn the volume waaaay down. That's what we want.)

■ **Be brave. Experiment.** I can only give you so much guidance from these pages; I'm not standing there in the middle of your arena, so I can't tell you, "You need more inside leg and inside flexion. There! That's enough!" So if you think you need a little more inside flexion or inside leg to prevent your horse from falling on his inside shoulder, try it. If you get no response, or too much, don't worry about it—he's more forgiving of honest mistakes than maybe you think. Besides, there's another corner coming right up where you can experiment again.

halting, bringing your horse's outside fore around, until the figure feels fluid, smooth, and symmetrical. Then change rein and ride the diamond tracking right until that feels just as good.

Ride the Octagon

Get set up: Following the diagram on page 38, use four additional cones to indicate the additional corners of the figure you're riding.

Now ride the pattern: Once again, ride straight to a point. A stride before, look ahead to the next point and prepare to take one or one-and-a-half strides to move your horse's outside shoulder up and around. The big difference? Because you're opening up the pattern, the turns are half as sharp, so they're a bit easier. But with eight turns instead of four, they're going to come up twice as fast. And your horse will start to look less completely straight on the straight sides and more consistently bent from poll to tail. When the octagon feels smooth, accurate, and secure in both directions, it's time to move right on and …

Ride the Circle

Get set up: You can either leave the traffic cones set up in the arena to guide you or take them away. (A hint: By now, you should have a pretty clear track you've created in the sand to follow.)

> If you've mastered the diamond, and you've mastered the octagon, the circle is going to be a piece of cake.

Now ride the pattern: The big difference from riding the diamond and the octagon? On the diamond, you moved your horse's outside shoulder up and around a fairly sharp square corner four times. On the octagon, you moved it up and around a more open corner eight times. Now you're going to smooth things out into what looks like one continuously curving line that starts and ends at the same place. You'll still ride to your points— and twelve, nine, six, and three o'clock are the most important ones. But by ever-so-slightly moving his shoulder up and around with every stride, you'll allow him to stay more consistently bent from poll to tail on the circular track. It will look like a perfect circle, it will feel like a perfect circle, and nobody but you and he will know that

you're still riding to points and turning very tiny corners by half-halting every stride and going "straight/turn/straight/turn/straight/turn."

And let me tell you something: If you've mastered the diamond, and you've mastered the octagon, the circle is going to be a piece of cake.

What If …

■ The corners come up too quickly for you to get organized? First ride the pattern at the walk. This will help make things as simple as possible for you and your horse. When you're comfortable and confident with your aids at the walk, then go ahead and try it at the trot. The idea here is to succeed, not to confuse and frustrate yourself or your horse.

■ You keep having trouble turning the corner and hitting the straight line to the next cone? Slow down and shorten your horse's trot stride so it's a very little bit under a working trot but he's still in front of your leg—in other words, he still wants to go forward, and you're not kicking all the time. This will make it easier to hit your points on the pattern.

■ Your horse drifts out on the corner? Use a stronger outside leg for three or four corners, or until he gets the idea that he can't drift out. Then back it off as much as you can—because your goal is always to get maximum response with a minimum of aids.

■ Your horse falls in on the corner? You've lost control of the balance in his shoulder. Focus more carefully on doing your aids by the number (look ahead, sit on your inside seat bone, flex him to the inside—which by now should rebalance him onto the outside shoulder—and half-halt). If this doesn't work, try going back a step or two in his training: Review flexing him in his jaw from the ground and at the standstill under saddle (as explained in Chapter 3).

■ You forget to look ahead at your next point or traffic cone? Having "eyes on the ground" never hurts, so ask a friend to come and remind you to maintain a pure rider position and to "look where you're going; look where you're going. You're two strides from E, so look at the centerline … Now you're two strides from the centerline, so look at B … You're approaching B, now look at the centerline. Before you get to the centerline, look over at E …" You'll then be ready for our next gymnastic exercise: Using the circle to spiff up your horse's transitions.

CHAPTER 6

GYMNASTIC EXERCISE 6:
TRANSITIONS

Combine a nearly perfect circle with timing and position to spiff up trot-to-canter and canter-to-trot transitions.

The quality of the gait—here, it's Cassiano's energetic, balanced canter—determines the quality of the transition, just as the quality of the transition almost always determines the quality of the gait.

As I PROMISED WHEN INTRODUCING the exercise in Chapter 5, a diamond you turned into an octagon and eventually into a circle, mastering it would give you control over the size and shape of all your circles. And that would pay off in all sorts of gymnasticizing figures, movements, and possibilities. In this lesson you'll enjoy one of those payoffs when we address the two transitions that I see riders and horses struggle with most: trot to canter and canter to trot.

I believe problems develop because these two transitions—of all the transitions between and within gaits—require you to change your rider position, moving your outside leg back from the hip to canter and forward to trot. (You do make the same position changes for canter/walk and walk/canter, but you won't get to those more technical transitions for a while, since they also require you to collect your horse and shorten his stride.) It can discombobulate you and confuse your horse if your aid:

■ Is timed incorrectly.
■ Disrupts your seat or other aids.

■ Is vague or unclear.
■ Distracts you from maintaining basic qualities like an inside flexion to your horse's jowl or a good, strong trot.

As a result, the transition may not happen. It can be muddled and inaccurate. It can be rough or abrupt. Your horse can lose the clear, three-beat tempo and rhythm of the canter, say, well before the moment when he actually drops into the trot. And rather than staying light in the hand, calm and correctly positioned going from trot to canter, he can get strong and crooked and end up barreling along like an express train.

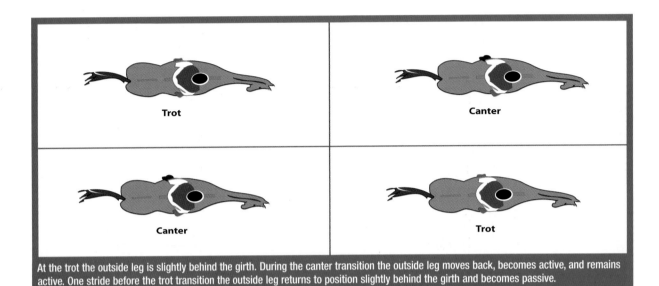

At the trot the outside leg is slightly behind the girth. During the canter transition the outside leg moves back, becomes active, and remains active. One stride before the trot transition the outside leg returns to position slightly behind the girth and becomes passive.

How Does the Circle Help?

It erases many of the troublesome variables that keep you from concentrating on your position and your aids. By now the circle is a familiar pattern, so your horse is confident about where he's going and you're not pulling on the reins to get there. The circle:

■ Gives you "place to be" so that if something goes wrong, you're not bouncing around the dressage arena like a pinball.

■ Makes it easier to maintain a soft inside flexion so you don't just pull on the outside corner of your horse's mouth when you half-halt. You apply rein pressure against the inside flexion, which allows the effect of the half-halt to travel all the way up and over your horse's poll and down his neck to his shoulder.

■ Makes it easier to keep your horse bent symmetrically from poll to tail around your inside leg, with his hind legs following in the track of his forelegs. Because of this flexion and bend, the circle encourages your horse to pick up the correct lead in the canter. And the qualities provided by a nearly perfect circle—rhythm, suppleness, balance, obedience—are the same qualities that make for a super transition.

Transitions Will Go Better If You:

■ Start working in the direction you and your horse are most comfortable. I'm going to talk you through them on the left rein, but that's simply because we photographed the exercise that way. If you and your horse are more comfortable trotting and cantering to the right, go that way first. But if you have trouble to the right, go back to the left and see if you don't get better results.

■ Carry a dressage whip in your outside hand. Yes, you customarily carry your whip on the inside to reinforce your inside driving aid. But if you carry it on the outside, and your horse doesn't respond by cantering when you put your outside leg back, you can immediately reinforce the aid with a tap. And if you feel him start to break from canter to trot while you still have your leg back, the whip will be there and ready to remind him he's still supposed to be cantering.

By the way, I never switch my whip at the moment I need to use it. The inevitable delay, even if it's only a second or two, means my horse is less liable to make the mental connection between his failure to respond and the correcting tap. Besides, if you get into the habit of tapping immediately upon switching your whip, your horse will quickly learn to spook whenever he feels or sees you beginning to change it. And you don't want that!

■ Sit the trot for two or three strides before asking for the canter depart. I've had you posting the trot until now—especially to help time your half-halts—but sitting is really the best way to get more seat and leg on your horse, increase communication and be deep in the saddle and ready for the first canter stride. But to be effective when you're sitting, you have to be comfortable.

So if your horse's working trot is so big or forward

> Transitions will go better if you carry a dressage whip in your outside hand.

Leg Aids for Trot and Canter

1 TROT: My outside leg is ever so slightly behind the girth when trotting on a circle (or asking for the canter/trot transition). I have full contact from my hip through my thigh and down into the upper part of my calf, which is the strongest part of my leg when riding. Note that even though I'm a dressage rider, I'm not using spurs because I want my horses to be as sensitive as possible to the lightest of seat and leg aids. I also want to be able to kick or thump to correct a horse without poking or hurting him. And more than anything, I never want to be tempted to use spurs instead of a classically correct position and leg aid. I always want my horses to respect spurs and not get so callused and dead to them from overuse that I have to ride with progressively bigger, longer, and sharper ones.

2 CANTER: When cantering (and asking for the trot/canter transition) on a circle, my outside leg is back from my hip all the way down through my knee and calf. Compare this with the trot photo and you can see that by bringing my outside hip back, I've also pushed my inside hip forward. This fairly exaggerated leg position is about the maximum you can do, and it's something you'd probably only need on a young or green horse.

Trot to Canter Transition

1 From the outside of this 20-meter circle, so that you can see my all-important outside aids, everything is ready for a smooth, responsive canter transition. Cassiano is in an energetic, quality, working trot. He has a nice inside left bend and flexion. My shoulders and hips are perpendicular to the track, my outside leg is a hair behind the girth, and I'm carrying my whip on the outside so I can immediately use it to reinforce my leg aid if needed. And I've just started two or three strides of sitting the trot.

2 The very next moment, I smoothly slide my outside leg back from hip to heel quite a bit more than normal for a made horse like Cassiano, just so you can really see the aid. I immediately give a half-halt by squeezing my outside right shoulder back and down a little, and I start to drive Cassiano into the canter by pushing my outside leg from hip to thigh against him as I swing my seat forward, and finally, give a rhythmic little squeeze with my inside leg.

3 Even though Cassiano's still finishing his last two-beat trot stride, he's already brought his outside right hind forward and is taking more weight on it to ...

4 Push off into the first full stride of a three-beat canter. I'm giving him all the encouragement I can by changing nothing. My hips and shoulders are still perpendicular to the track. My seat is swinging in the canter rhythm. My hands are close together and even. There's a straight line from my elbow to the bit. And my outside leg is back where it will stay, saying "canter" until I'm ready to ask Cassiano to trot again.

that you bounce or get unbalanced, temporarily slow the trot a bit, just as I had you do on the circle pattern in the last chapter, as long as your horse stays nicely active and in front of your leg (your ultimate goal is to stay in the working trot).

Having said this, I believe it is very important to teach your horse that sitting is not the aid for the canter transition. Lay that groundwork by trotting around the circle several times, alternately posting three or four strides and sitting three or four strides. (This is also a great way to practice your sitting trot, because you get to post before you start to bounce or fall apart.) Be sure to stay consistent. If you slow your horse's trot to sit, keep the same, slow tempo and rhythm when you post. If your posting trot is forward and energetic, stay just as forward when you sit.

■ Bring your entire outside leg back from the hip, all the way from your seatbone to your thigh and into your calf (instead of just raising your heel as I see many riders do). Whether your horse does dressage, jumpers, eventing, or equitation, when he starts to understand that your

> How far back is "back"? I tell my students it is "as far back as you have to take it to make sure your horse really feels and understands the aid."

outside leg back from the hip means a canter transition, he's well on his way to understanding "keep cantering until I bring it forward again." And when that light bulb turns on, you've opened the door to such transitions and movements as working canter to lengthened canter and back, counter-canter (where you deliberately ask your horse to canter on the "wrong" lead), flying changes, half-passes, even canter pirouettes.

How far back is "back"? I tell my students it is "as far back as you have to take it to make sure your horse really feels and understands the aid." For now, while you and he are mastering this new seat and leg position, that may be as much as six to eight inches behind the girth. As you and he get more experienced, you can bring your leg back less and less.

■ Make your canter/trot half-halt on the inside rein. I know that classical horsemen may roll their eyes at this, but half-halting on the inside rein effectively stops your horse's inside hind from swinging forward while he is

cantering, so he naturally drops into the trot. It will also clearly differentiate canter/trot from canter/walk and canter/halt (for which you half-halt on the outside rein) when you start doing them later on.

Ready? Let's get right to work.

Trot to Canter Transition

Pick up an energetic posting trot on a 20-meter circle tracking left. Sit square in the saddle, with your hips and shoulders perpendicular to the track. Keep your inside left "driving" leg at the girth and, because you're on a circle, your outside right leg a hair behind the girth. Check that your horse is softly flexed around your inside left rein, evenly bent around your inside left leg from the tip of his poll to the tip of his tail, and listening and responding to the half-halts on your outside (right) rein. Above all, make sure the quality of your trot is good. I know I've said it before, but it bears repeating: The quality of the trot is going to determine the quality of the transition.

Now ask for the canter. Sit the trot, and in the first trot stride, make sure he's softly flexed to the inside. In the next trot stride, without squeezing or pushing, slide your entire outside (right) leg back. In the next stride, half-halt (squeeze your outside right shoulder back and slightly down) to "lift and pause" your horse's outside right shoulder and fore-leg. In that same moment, squeeze and push with your outside leg and seat to drive your horse's haunches up underneath him, especially the outside right hind leg so it will be able to strike off into the first step of the canter stride.

The feeling you want to have is that you squeeze and drive with your outside leg, but the drive travels from your outside hip through to your inside seatbone, in very much the same motion you make when using your seat to accelerate a swing. This pushes your inside hip forward toward your horse's outside ear. I tell my students, "Even though you're still technically perpendicular to the track, imagine that a beam of light is shooting out of your inside hip bone, and you're shining that light on your horse's outside ear."

Once you have the canter, continue the rhythmic swing in your seat. Your inside rein is still your flexion rein. Your outside rein is still your half-halting rein. Your inside leg is still your driving leg. None of that has changed. The only thing that's different is that your outside leg stays back so that the swing in your seat travels from your outside hip to your inside hip. Now enjoy the feeling of cantering on for a while. Don't get hasty about doing a downward transition. Instead, run through your "quality checklist" to make sure the canter feels balanced and rhythmic, even if that takes two or three times around in the beginning. Then, and only then, ask for a ...

Canter-to-Trot Transition

Smoothly, in one motion and without hesitation, relax your outside leg and bring it forward to just a hair behind the girth. In almost the same moment, half-halt on the inside left rein: Maintain contact on the outside right rein, but without changing the flexion to the right

> If you try and try and really struggle, seek qualified professional help before you and your horse become totally frustrated.

as you would for a classical half-halt. Then squeeze your left inside shoulder back and down, not enough to increase flexion or bend to the inside, but just enough to tell your horse to stop his inside hind from swinging forward in the canter and step down into a trot. As soon as you feel that two-beat trot, tell him, "Yes, trot," by letting your seat pick up the two-beat rhythm. Sit for a few strides, then post.

Problem Solving

Trot/canter transition: If your horse doesn't respond, exaggerate your aids. Really move your outside leg way back from your hip, do a stronger half-halt, and give a thump with your heel or a tap with the whip. If he trots bigger, faster and longer instead of cantering, first restore the quality of the trot. (Unless you're a really good rider, you can't kick a horse into a canter from a big, booming trot.) Smoothly bring your outside leg forward and give as strong a half-halt as necessary to bring him back to a working trot. Then try again. If he picks up the canter, then canters a few strides and breaks to trot, remind him that as long as your outside leg is back, it means "canter." Keep your outside leg back, half-halt and immediately kick or tap him into the canter again.

Canter/trot transition: If your horse responds,

but his trot is big and booming like a freight train, immediately start posting so you can stay relaxed and effective. (Do not halt or walk. Your horse can get frustrated and throw his head up or even try to rear a little. He may quickly learn to suck behind your leg. And he could interpret it as a reward instead of a correction.) Make sure you have a nice inside flexion, because when a horse starts racing, he often loses—or takes away from you—the inside flexion and bend.

Have the confidence to make him match a much slower tempo in your seat and stay in front of your leg, in other words, still forward and energetic. Tell him, "Hey! I want a nice, relaxed, listening trot, not that frantic, running-away thing." Or go back to a gymnastic pattern like the shallow serpentine that will focus his attention because it's familiar. Once you're satisfied that he's listening, make it your idea to ask him to go more forward into a working trot again.

Need more help? If you try and try and really struggle, seek qualified professional help before you and your horse become totally frustrated. I can't tell you how many times I've gotten on a student's horse, schooled a transition several times, put my student back on and not only had the transition work, but both rider and horse felt the aids and the timing, and they went on successfully from there.

Take It Up A Notch

I've told you to trot or canter until you're satisfied with the quality of the gait, but as you start to get organized faster and your horse understands better, work on improving accuracy, response and smoothness. Your goal, which will help you immeasurably in the show ring: a prompt canter transition at B; a balanced, rhythmic canter halfway around the circle with an accurate trot transition at E; a balanced, organized trot halfway around the circle; a canter exactly at B and so on.

Increase the challenge with transitions on straight lines where you don't have the circle to help you. Canter across the diagonal on the right lead, say, trot at X, trot to K and between K and A, where you still have the support of a curving track, pick up the new left lead. Canter a left-lead circle between B and E. At B, go straight, and on the long side between B and M, trot. Finally, canter across the diagonal and do a change of leads through the trot over X.

Canter to Trot Transition

1 Cassiano takes the last step of the canter stride on his inside fore, and as his haunches start to come forward ...

2 I relax my outside leg, slide it forward to the girth area and, maintaining the inside flexion and bend, half-halt on the inside by squeezing my left shoulder back and down a little, which has really allowed my seat to sink down and around. Even though I'm holding a little longer on the inside rein, my position hasn't changed. Now that I feel that Cassiano has broken the three-beat canter and is getting into the two-beat trot ...

3 I will sit this very nice working trot for a few strides, maintaining the inside flexion and bend on the inside rein and half-halting on the outside rein, then go back to posting.

Wrong Techniques For Transitions

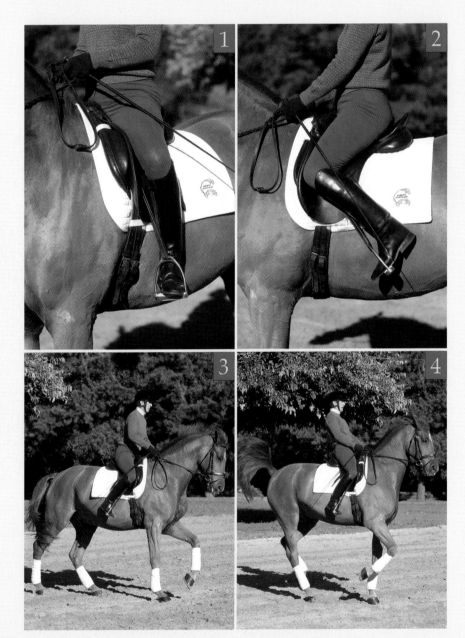

1 If I ask for the canter by sticking my heel into Cassiano's side, I collapse and tilt onto my inside seatbone. My outside thigh lifts off the saddle and my knee rolls out, which makes my leg weaker and less effective. This makes my foot turn out as well, so instead of my weight resting evenly across the ball of my entire foot, all the pressure is on my little toe.

2 If I ask for the canter by raising my heel and bringing my lower leg back from the knee, I pull my seat out of the saddle, tip forward, and completely lose the benefit of my strong upper calf. If Cassiano were to stumble or buck, I'm so insecure that I'd fly right over his head.

3 By leaning forward in hopes of egging Cassiano on into the canter, I've pulled my seat out of the saddle and I've lost the ability to half-halt. In addition, I've swung my lower leg back and up, so there's no driving strength in my leg. I'm also unbalanced and tilting to the inside. The result? Even though Cassiano has cantered, he looks annoyed and the quality of the transition and resulting canter are pretty poor. (Compare this flat, strung-out canter depart with the round depart in Photo 3 in the "Trot-To-Canter Transition" box on Page 46, where he's really lifting in front).

4 Instead of bringing my outside leg forward and asking for the trot transition by half-halting, I've left my outside leg back and I'm leaning back against both reins equally and hauling on Cassiano's mouth. As a result, he has no flexion to the inside (he's nearly flexed to the outside), and once again is a very confused and unhappy camper. And there's been NO downward transition!

CHAPTER 7

GYMNASTIC EXERCISE 7:
TURN ON THE FOREHAND

Introduce your horse
to the idea of moving
sideways with this
useful exercise.

As my ground person, Bettina is helping me to move Montero's haunches to the right, developing the turn on the forehand.

YOUR HORSE NOW KNOWS how to move forward and back in response to your seat and leg. He turns and changes direction in response to your balance and weight. He flexes, responds to half-halts, makes accurate circles, and does spiffy trot-to-canter and canter-to-trot transitions. With these skills under his belt, he can start thinking about moving laterally, or sideways. You'll introduce this idea at the halt with "turn on the forehand," where he responds to direct inside leg pressure by moving his haunches around his forehand in an arc.

What Turn on the Forehand Accomplishes

This useful schooling exercise (not a movement you'll see in any dressage test) supples your horse, increases his obedience to your aids, and establishes the basic building block for such show-ring lateral work as leg-yield and shoulder-in. Turn on the forehand benefits you by increasing your ability to keep your horse flexed consis-

tently through figures and movements. It improves your control over the shape of turns, circles, and figures and fine-tunes your feel for how and when he responds to your aids and with which leg or legs.

Before we go further, I must tell you that turn on the forehand isn't the only way to introduce lateral movement. Many skillful and classical trainers use leg-yield, where your horse walks or trots forward AND sideways, on the theory that influencing your horse is usually easier when he's in motion, especially if you're

Begin by flexing the horse's jaw to the right and then apply an active right leg to move the haunches to the left. The rider is looking for an immediate response to the rider's leg.

■ A helper can do what I do when I teach turn on the forehand to a student for the first time. He or she can stand next to your horse, put one hand on your inside calf and the other on your horse's inside hip and calmly, quietly, but precisely, reinforce and clarify your sideways aids with a push. (Staying beside you both at a trot or even a brisk walk would be quite a challenge!) And that helper can be anybody—your grandmother, a friend, the postman—as long as he or she is there to clarify your aids and calm and reassure your horse.

What You'll Do

Because turn on the forehand is very much an obedience exercise, you'll ask your horse for one sideways stride—four walk beats or footfalls—at a time. He should stand still until you ask him to move, but his response when you do should be as sharp and prompt as a halt/walk or trot/canter transition. He should initiate each stride by crossing his inside hind diagonally forward in front of his outside hind. Then, just as if he were walking straight ahead, he should clearly and distinctly lift and put down his other feet in turn.

He'll complete the stride with his hind feet having moved one step sideways in an arc around his forehand, and his forefeet having turned and just barely moved forward. Then you'll halt for three to five seconds. You'll ask for two more four-step strides and halts, then you'll give him a long rein and walk off.

But that's the ideal. In practice, especially while the two of you are figuring things out, his first response as he thinks about your direct inside calf pressure may be sluggish. He may take a big sideways step with his outside hind first, rather than his inside hind. He may be an overachiever who swings his haunches away in several sideways steps instead of just one. He may take a big step or two forward. Or he may commit the significant no-no of planting his inside fore and kind of "screwing" it into the ground as he turns.

These exaggerated or confused responses are OK for now, as long as he moves his haunches sideways away

trying to influence him in a new, unfamiliar way. I use turn on the forehand before I attempt leg-yielding at the walk. I've found that turn on the forehand works best in my program because ...

■ You start from the halt, which automatically establishes a low-key, low-stress atmosphere.

■ With your horse's mind quiet, he can confidently focus on your aids and the new information you're giving him. He's less likely to get confused or upset as he might when he's in motion. In fact, his comfort level should be high because he's already learned something new at the halt: flexing, bending and softening his jaw. (See Chapter 3.)

> Because turn on the forehand is very much an obedience exercise, you'll ask your horse for one sideways stride—four walk beats or footfalls—at a time.

■ Without the distracting issues of balance and seat that often arise when your horse is going forward, you are better able to concentrate on the feel and especially the timing of your aids and zoom in on when and how he reacts and responds to them.

from your direct inside leg pressure. With time and experience, he'll figure things out and tone things down, and you'll get better at controlling every step. The one mistake he is never allowed to make is backing up, because he's dropping behind your leg and is no longer forward thinking.

Now Ride the Exercise

First, find a spot near the center of the arena where you and your horse have plenty of elbow room to make a turn and you won't get in the way of other riders if they're schooling. If your arena is equipped with mirrors, I strongly recommend you use them to see how and when your horse is moving his feet. If you have a friend helping you, ask her to stand facing you on your left side, with her left hand resting lightly on your calf and her right hand resting lightly on your horse's hipbone. You're going to move him sideways off your left leg as I talk you through this exercise.

At the halt, check your position. Make sure you're sitting balanced on both seat bones, with a tall upper body and your weight dropping down into your heels. Because you're going to move sideways to the right, ask for a slight inside, left flexion by turning the knuckles of

Turn on the Forehand With a Helper

1 My assistant, Bettina, softly rests her left hand on my left calf and her right hand on Montero's left hipbone. I press with my inside, left calf to ask Montero to move his haunches sideways. When he doesn't respond she immediately pushes on my calf and his hipbone as she steps into him. And now he gets it! He moves sideways by crossing his left hind in front of his right hind. Note that Bettina is keeping an eye on Montero's feet because as soon as ...

2 ... he responds, she takes her hands away (and just as if I were alone, I relax my inside leg). If she kept pushing, he'd probably continue moving to the right, but instead, he starts to bring his right hind around to square it up next to his left.

Turn on the Forehand on Your Own

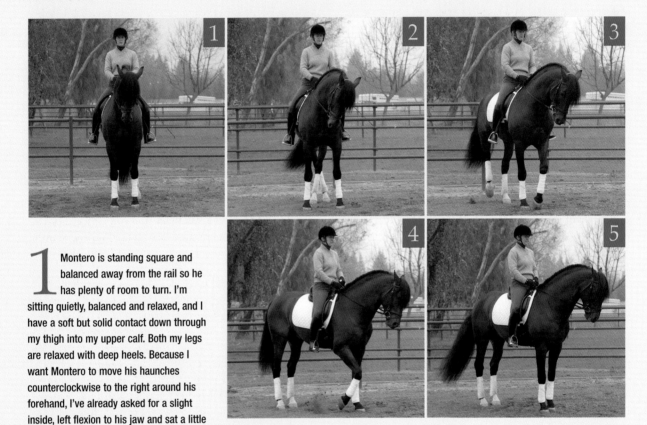

1 Montero is standing square and balanced away from the rail so he has plenty of room to turn. I'm sitting quietly, balanced and relaxed, and I have a soft but solid contact down through my thigh into my upper calf. Both my legs are relaxed with deep heels. Because I want Montero to move his haunches counterclockwise to the right around his forehand, I've already asked for a slight inside, left flexion to his jaw and sat a little bit deeper on my left seat bone.

2 I slide my inside, left leg slightly back from the girth and press my calf against Montero's side to ask him to move his haunches to the right. And he obliges with the response we're all searching for by crossing his left hind in front of his right hind. My right, outside leg is still passively "there" telling him he can freely take this one step. It's also ready to act as a wall to stop his haunches from swinging away from my left leg. I am definitely sitting deeper on my inside seat bone, but without sacrificing the rest of my position, which is still upright, square, and still. Montero has dropped a little behind the vertical, but that's OK because he's still softly flexed to the left and giving me a good, honest contact.

3 I tell Montero I want no more sideways movement by releasing the pressure on my inside, left leg and half-halting on my outside, right rein. In very short order, but still within the distinct rhythm of a four-beat walk, he brings his right hind around and is just about to set it down next to his left hind as he starts lifting his left fore and taking a small, straightening step forward.

4 For the final step, Montero lifts his outside, right fore and moves it a little forward to square up next to the left.

5 Then he stands still and square. I've slightly softened the left flexion, and although my inside left leg is still slightly back, both my legs are relaxed and quietly hanging down at his side. Because turn on the forehand is very much an obedience exercise, we'll just stand here and settle for about three to five seconds. Then I'll start all over again, first by asking for a bit more inside flexion, then by pressing my inside calf against his side again. Because this gymnastic pattern is a little static and I always want my horses to be forward thinking, I'll ask one more time, for a total of three, four-step strides and halts, then slide my inside leg forward and soften the flexion, and we'll walk off on a long rein and do something else.

your left hand toward your right hip. By now your horse should pretty reliably yield to this direct pressure by lowering his poll, softening in the jowl area (the crease where his head joins his neck), relaxing his jaw and coming softly on the bit.

To me, "on the bit" is less about his face being precisely on the vertical than it is about him listening and giving and accepting a soft contact. At the same time you ask him to flex, sink a penny's worth more weight onto your left seat bone and down into your left leg. Stay relaxed and loose in the saddle so your seat clearly tells your horse, "Stay here. Stand still. I'm not asking you to go forward."

Slightly soften the contact on your outside, right rein to give him room to turn to the right, and allow your outside, right leg to lie passively there on his side, ready to be a wall that keeps his haunches from overreacting

> To me, "on the bit" is less about his face being precisely on the vertical than it is about him listening and giving and accepting a soft contact.

and swinging wide or taking several sideways steps. But don't press or squeeze with your right leg or you could really confuse and frustrate your horse by inadvertently telling him to go both ways at once.

Bring your left, inside leg back just a little bit behind the girth and squeeze and press your calf against your horse's side to ask him to take his haunches one step to the right.

If he doesn't respond and you have a helper, immediately have her step into him and push against your calf and his hip, but only after your horse has failed to move off your leg. Your goal is always to have him respond to your aid. If you're on your own, lift your left leg an inch or two away from his side and give him a little thump that says, "Hey, wake up. I know this is a new idea, but I asked you to move over." If he still doesn't get it, touch or tickle him behind your calf with your dressage whip. Do no more than that. If you get rowdy and start whacking, you'll cause more problems than you'll ever solve. As with all training, keeping your horse calm is your top priority. Whenever he gets upset or excited, he stops listening and learning.

As soon as he starts to take that first step, even if it's

with the less-than-ideal outside hind, tell him that's all the sideways movement you want. "Catch" his foot in mid-air by simultaneously relaxing your inside leg, which is still back, to a passive contact and half-halting on your outside, right rein. If you have a helper, she should lift both hands completely away. Your horse should set his foot down and complete the single stride of turn on the forehand by squaring up his other feet and going no further. Your timing will be very much a judgment call. If your horse tends to move like molasses, you probably won't relax your leg and half-halt until his inside hind is almost back on the ground. If he's a quick-moving little jumping bean, you may need to relax and half-halt as soon as his inside hind starts to lift.

How will you know your horse has taken four steps? You should be able to feel them. You can glance down at his shoulders to confirm that he's squared up and straight. If you have a mirror, you can watch and check them. Or if you have a helper, she can tell you.

Now, how long do you stand at the halt? Under ordinary circumstances, I suggest three to five seconds. But if your horse seems confused or his mind is starting to work faster than it should, take more time settling and reassuring him before asking again. Repeat this sequence no more than twice, then allow his nose to straighten up, bring your inside leg back toward the girth and give a push with your seat and a squeeze with your legs to ask him to walk forward.

Finally, give him a long rein and pat him to really let him know that he was very, very good. Do a bit of free walk around the arena and come across the diagonal. Then gather up the reins, work your way back into the center and ask for a turn on the forehand to the left.

What if ...

■ ... your horse keeps stepping back? I guarantee that either he's not softly on the bit, you have too much feel of his mouth or you're leaning forward, so your seat bones are actually pushing him back.

Don't believe me? Try it right now. Put down this book, slide your hands, palm up, under your seat bones, then tip forward and feel how your pushing-back seat bones could be unintentionally telling your horse "step back." Check your contact, make sure your horse is flexed to the inside and even give a little push with your seat to remind him to go a little bit forward as he turns.

■ ... he persistently walks forward? Without putting more pressure on the reins, ask for a little more inside, left flexion. Or try the turn facing into a wall or a fence. Because your horse has to move somewhere and he can't go forward, he'll be more inclined to go sideways.

■ ... he fidgets at the halt? (Or throws his head when you ask him to flex his jaw?) Put turn on the forehand on the shelf for now because it's not going to work. Instead, go back to Chapter 3 and use Exercise 3 until he can stay calm, quiet, and attentive while halting, flexing, and bending.

■ ... he becomes really upset and flustered? If you haven't

already done so, now is the time to bring in a helper who can clarify your aids and calm and reassure your horse.

■ ... you're just not making progress in the arena? Use turn on the forehand to open and shut a gate. With my bad knee, it's something I teach all my horses because I don't want to have to dismount and mount again just to get into or out of a paddock, corral, arena, or pasture. But I've found that working a gate also clarifies exactly what I want a horse to do because it gives him a "mission."

Wrong!

1 A classic turn on the forehand mistake: My inside hand is high and crossing over Montero's withers and my outside right arm is so straight (my fingers are even open) that I'm completely giving up all contact on the right. As a result, Montero is overflexed with his nose well past the point of his shoulder and his neck off to the side. His body is no longer straight and, instead of being balanced onto his right shoulder, he's leaning all his weight in that direction, which is just going to make the turn that much harder.

2 My hands are chest high, I'm crossing my left hand over Montero's withers and I've raised my heel and tipped forward. He is so confused and irritated, he tosses his head, pins his ears and, instead of turning, backs up.

CHAPTER 8

GYMNASTIC EXERCISE 8:
SPIRAL-IN & SPIRAL-OUT

Straighten and rebalance
your horse by gradually
decreasing and increasing
the size of a 20-meter circle.

Ride this simple gymnastic pattern once or twice every schooling session, and you'll make your horse more supple, obedient, and adjustable.

HAVING MASTERED TURN ON the forehand (Chapter 7), your horse understands how to move sideways away from your leg from the standstill. He's now ready to start moving off your leg while he's in motion. To introduce this skill, you're going to spiral in and spiral out on a circle just like a needle spiraling on a phonograph record (for those of you who are old enough to know what that is).

I have to tell you, this is my very favorite gymnastic exercise. It's straightforward and simple, but it's a schooling powerhouse. I use spiral-in and spiral-out every day in some way with every horse I ride. On the green horses, I do the no-frills version that I'm going to teach you. (With youngsters not yet under saddle, I use it on the longe). On my more advanced horses, I increase the gymnasticizing effect by throwing in transitions as I ride the pattern or I do it in shoulder-in, renvers, or haunches-in, even counter-canter. And on my Grand Prix horse, Cassiano, I spiral in and out in the very collected, very elevated, and very cadenced trot known as passage.

Here's What You'll Do

With your horse evenly bent to the inside from poll to tail, you'll start to reduce the diameter of a 20-meter circle. You'll ask him to bring his outside foreleg up and across so he puts it down inside of the track he was on (I'll describe how you do this in a moment). It will feel as if for one step, and one step only, his forehand slightly leads his haunches, which immediately cross over and catch up. You'll continue to repeat this sequence until you've gradually spiraled in to a circle that's about 12 to 15 meters in diameter.

To spiral out and increase the size of the circle, you'll

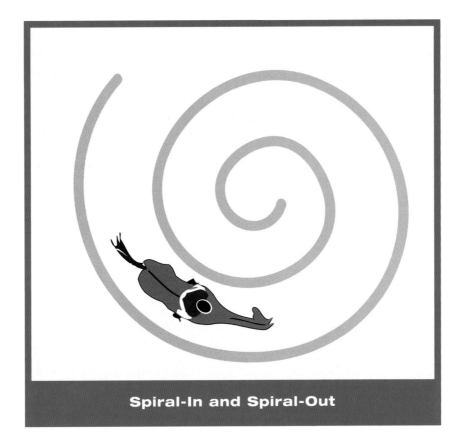

Spiral-In and Spiral-Out

Here's What You'll Accomplish

■ **You'll make your horse straight.** And when I say "straight" I mean that whether he's going down the long side or he's bending around a 10-meter half-circle, his hind feet follow exactly in line with his front feet. His chest is perpendicular to the track he's moving on and "looking" where he's going. And his spine is evenly shaped from poll to tail according to the arc of the track.

■ **You'll supple him.** By gradually increasing and decreasing the size of the circle, he'll gradually and smoothly increase and decrease the poll-to-tail inside bend through his body.

■ **You'll rebalance him.** To spiral in, he has to raise and lighten his shoulders, which automatically puts more weight and balance on his haunches. To spiral out, he has to step under and across with his inside hind, which again causes him to distribute his balance rearward and carry more weight on his haunches.

■ **You'll detect problems.** As you go in and out to the right and the left, you'll be able to contrast and compare and feel which way your horse is a little stiffer or more crooked. And good news—through repetition, the pattern will soften his stiffer side (spend more time riding the pattern that way) and rebalance him laterally so he's straighter.

■ **You'll increase adjustability.** I tell my students that everything in the dressage arena can boil down to a little spiral-in or spiral-out. If your horse feels as if he's become a little crooked because he's shifted his haunches into the arena when he's cantering down the long side, an imperceptible step of spiral-out will straighten him. If he's leaning into his outside shoulder going through a corner, a tiny step of spiral-in will rebalance and get him properly aligned.

ask your horse to cross his inside hind under and across toward his outside shoulder about one step's width. The effect: His haunches will ever so slightly lead his forehand for one footfall before his forehand catches up. Again he'll repeat this sequence until the circle is back to 20 meters in diameter.

> I tell my students that everything in the dressage arena can boil down to a little spiral-in or spiral-out.

Although this description of the spiral-in and spiral-out may sound disjointed or herky-jerky, the exercise is anything but. When you do it correctly, your horse stays technically straight and evenly bent to the inside and the whole pattern looks smooth, balanced, and seamless. He never leans on his inside shoulder going in. He never falls on his outside shoulder going out (I'll explain why none of this happens in a moment).

And believe me, this kind of maneuverability isn't just for dressage horses. A step or two of spiral-in can help a jumper shave seconds off his round. An equitation horse that can spiral out will make better-balanced turns. Even a hunter under saddle who gets stuck behind another horse on the rail can seamlessly spiral in a step or two, pass and spiral back out again.

Spiraling Do's and Don'ts

DO decrease and increase gradually, taking about half a circle—from E to B, say—to spiral in or out about one meter. And if, at any time, you run into problems because your horse is crooked, losing his balance, or changing his tempo, STOP spiraling and stay on the circle until he's straight, balanced, and maintaining the speed you want.

DON'T go so small your horse loses balance and impulsion. Rather than having me give you a specific number that may or may not suit your horse, just let his gaits, age, balance, and size dictate the size of the circle. As long as he maintains engagement, impulsion, and an even bend from poll to tail, you're OK.

Spiral-In

1 As you can see from the track in the sand, we're partway around the spiral pattern. I've relaxed into the saddle and softened my rein and leg aids in this sitting phase of the posting trot (Picasso's inside fore and outside hind are in flight). I'm square and erect, my hips and shoulders are perpendicular to the circular track we're on, and my eyes are looking slightly in where we're going.

Because I want Picasso to move away from my outside leg and rein, I'm carrying my whip in my outside hand. His trot is energetic and forward. I'd like to see a bit more right bend and flexion, but I'm not overly concerned. Straightening like this is a typical "green" response to my active outside leg and rein, and it will go away with practice. For now, I know I can reestablish the flexion and bend in the next stride, so I'm not going to do what I recommend to you: Stop spiraling and go straight on the circle until everything's fixed.

2 In the next step, I've regained the inside bend and flexion so Picasso's hips are once again following his shoulders. Because this is the upbeat of the trot stride, I'm asking him to take a spiral-in step by applying a little stronger outside leg. I'm half-halting on the outside rein and lightly pressing it against Picasso's left shoulder, but without crossing my left hand over his withers. He's responding nicely by bringing his outside foreleg inside the track from shoulder to hoof.

3 In the next phase of the trot stride, Picasso's a bit farther in on the pattern and nicely bent around my inside leg as I relax my aids and sit again.

DO ride the pattern at the rising trot. Later you can sit the trot and also do it at the walk and canter, but while you're learning, posting will help you time your aids. Remember, every time you rise out of the saddle, your horse's outside fore and inside hind are in flight, and that's when you can influence them with your seat and half-halts.

DON'T overdo. In general, I ride this pattern once each way during a schooling session. While you're learning, of course, you may want to practice it more than that. That's OK as long as you keep it fresh by interspersing it with other work and riding it in different areas of the arena.

DO add this pattern to your longe work, but spiral-in no smaller than 15 meters. Smaller than that will put too much stress on your horse's legs and make it too hard for him to maintain bend, gait, and balance.

DON'T be embarrassed to ask a friend to serve as your "eyes on the ground." Believe me, everybody needs that (I rarely get on a horse without my assistant watching). She can tell you what you can't always feel or be aware of: That maybe your horse isn't straight, his inside hind isn't crossing under his body, or his chest is looking to the outside.

DO remember the tools you've developed with

Spiral-Out

1 We've gone around once or twice on the smallest circle of the pattern, and now we're ready to spiral out. This, again, is the downbeat of the trot stride, so I'm sitting and relaxing my aids and Picasso has a nice little flexion to the inside. Why am I carrying my whip on the left when I would ordinarily want it on the right to reinforce my inside aids? For some reason, when you say "spiral out" on this pattern, most horses fall apart, lean into their outside shoulder and zoom toward the rail. The whip in my outside hand and in front of my knee is ready in case I need to tap Picasso on the shoulder and say, "Hey. Stay straight."

2 In the next step, the upbeat, I ask Picasso to move his haunches out a bit. I press my inside right leg into him to ask him to move his inside right hind diagonally across and underneath himself toward his straight, forward-reaching, left outside shoulder (compare the position of his leg and shoulder here with that in the same moment of spiral-in; photo 2, page 59). Note that I'm still sitting upright, square, and perpendicular to the track, and as much as I'm using my inside leg, my heel is down and my weight is still down in my stirrups.

3 This is a really nice moment. As Picasso starts the next step on the downbeat, he's just beginning to bring his outside hind up and around his crossed-under inside hind, which will automatically complete the spiral-out stride with him slightly farther out on the pattern. He's also nicely bent and straight from poll to tail with a soft inside flexion in his jowl.

previous gymnastic patterns. You KNOW how to ride a 20-meter circle. You KNOW how to half-halt. And if your horse slows down as he spirals in, you KNOW how to use your seat and leg to push him forward again.

Spiral-In

Tracking right on a 20-meter circle, pick up an energetic posting trot. Sit square and tall in the saddle, with your shoulders and hips perpendicular to the 20-meter track. Keep your outside leg a hair behind the girth—just enough to encourage your horse to bend around your inside leg, which is at the girth. Ask for a soft inside flexion in your horse's right jowl by quietly turning your right knuckles toward your outside left hip. And make sure he's on the bit, which means he's listening and giving you a soft, elastic, conversational contact.

Circle a few times or until the figure feels easy, smooth, and symmetrical and your horse has a nice, steady, quality trot that's neither running and hurried nor lazy and slow. Memorize that trot. It's very important as you ride the pattern to make sure the tempo and rhythm stay the same.

> The big difference: Spiraling in, your horse moved his forehand in first. Spiraling out, you're going to ask him to move his haunches out first by stepping his inside right hind under and across toward his outside left shoulder.

When the circle feels good, start gradually spiraling in one step at a time. As you rise, ask your horse to bring his outside left foreleg, which is in flight, a step inward to the right. Press your outside left leg into him from your hip down to the top of your calf. Half-halt on your outside left rein by squeezing your outside shoulder back and down so the rein comes a little back and also by slightly pressing it against your horse's neck. It should feel almost as if you're using the rein to "push" his shoulder over and around onto the track of a slightly smaller circle, without crossing it over the withers—which you should never do.

As you sit, relax your rein and leg aids, then just maintain them as you trot straight a stride or two. Then ask your horse to come in another step, until you've taken about half a circle to spiral in about one meter. Continue the pattern in this manner, going only to as

small a circle as your horse can negotiate without losing balance, impulsion, or bend. Circle once or twice on the small circle, then ask him to ...

Spiral-Out

Again, you want your horse to stay technically straight; in other words, evenly bent from poll to tail according to the arc of the circle he's on. You still want him on the bit with a soft inside flexion in his jowl. You still want to go out one step at a time. And if it took you five times around to come in on the spiral, you want to take five times around—not three, or two, or seven—to get back out again.

The big difference: Spiraling in, your horse moved his forehand in first. Spiraling out, you're going to ask him to move his haunches out first by stepping his inside right hind under and across toward his outside left shoulder (very much the way he did while turning on the forehand in Chapter 7). The feeling will be that he's slightly leading with his haunches. If he leads with his outside shoulder, he'll no longer be bent from poll to tail according to the arc of the circle and he'll fall out on the pattern.

Bring your inside right leg slightly back behind the girth and as you rise, press it from your hip down to the top part of your calf against your horse's side to ask him to step across and under. At the same time, give a half-halting squeeze with your outside shoulder on the left rein to momentarily block his outside shoulder from leaning or bulging and to pause it in flight. By the time it does come down, it will be aligned in front of his outside hind again. As you sit, soften your half-halting rein and inside leg. Maintain those aids as you trot straight for a stride or two, then ask for another step of spiral-out. Repeat this sequence until you reach a 20-meter circle. Circle once or twice, then go off around the arena and change the subject.

What If ...

- **Confusion reigns.** Your horse gets confused when you put your leg on and instead of moving sideways, he squirts forward? My first recommendation is to go back and clarify the difference between your forward-moving and sideways-moving leg aids, devoting a little more time to working on forward and back (see Chapter 1, page 7) and turn on the forehand (Chapter 7, page 51).

After that, just stop asking your horse to spiral, stay on the circle and use stronger half-halts to reestablish rhythm, tempo, and the quality of the trot before continuing.

■ **Anticipation rules.** Your horse anticipates, takes over, and zooms from 20 to 15 meters in one stride? My mentor, Olympic three-day coach Erich Bubbel, used to define anticipation as your horse (in those days, it was MY horse) not being on the aids! One reason this lesson's exercise should be gradual is to help you develop control over every stride.

So increase that control, get your horse back on the aids, and cure his tendency to anticipate by playing with the spiral pattern. Keep him guessing so he can't say, "Oh! I know what we're doing." Don't always spiral in to the smallest circle you can ride—let's say it's 15 meters. Instead, go in to 17 meters, circle, go out to 19, circle, go in to 15, circle, go out to 18, and so on. It's up to you to make those decisions about how to get your horse totally listening, responding, and on the aids. But, hey, that is going to be soooo much fun.

■ **There's a lean.** Your horse leans or bulges into his shoulder and falls out? You're not alone. More often than not, when I stand in the middle of a circle and teach this gymnastic pattern to a student, she pretty much gets the coming-in part. But the minute I say, "OK, now spiral back out," she lets her horse's shoulders go and she's literally trotting away from me! So be very aware of making your horse take the first step out with his inside hind. Even if you don't feel him leaning or bulging into his shoulder, you or your eyes-on-the-ground helper will see that the front of his chest, between the points of his shoulders, is no longer perpendicular to the track but is turned and looking outward. Immediately circle until your horse is straight again. And check to make sure YOUR hips and shoulders are still perpendicular to the track. Then continue the pattern, but know that you probably need to use firmer outside half-halts to keep that shoulder in line.

Wrong!

I'm trying to spiral out, but I have too much pressure on the inside rein. Instead of pushing Picasso where I want him to go with my seat, I'm trying to pull him there with the rein. As a result, he's overbent through his head and neck, which is making him fall out over his outside shoulder off the pattern. His outside fore, instead of pointing straight ahead as it did in Spiral-out photo 2, page 60, is pointing out of the pattern over THERE! To complicate matters, I'm twisted and uneven in the saddle, with my weight to the left, my right hand crossing over the withers and my outside half-halting shoulder and hip forward instead of back.

To fix this mess, I'd forget about spiraling out and think, "CIRCLE!" Only when I'd reestablished bend and balance would I ask Picasso to spiral out again, but this time I'd think, "Push the haunches out."

CHAPTER 9

GYMNASTIC EXERCISE 9:
THREE-LOOP SERPENTINE

Develop suppleness, strength, and balance with this useful pattern.

A three-loop serpentine is made up of three 20-meter half-circle loops that touch and change direction at the centerline.

YOU TAUGHT YOUR HORSE TO CHANGE his bend and balance while he's standing still (Chapter 3). You perfected the 20-meter circle (Chapter 5). And in Chapter 8 you increased maneuverability and obedience with spiral-in and spiral-out. In this lesson you'll build on all those skills by riding a symmetrical three-loop serpentine made up of three 20-meter half-circle loops that touch and change direction at the centerline. (See diagram on page 64).

This exercise adds a degree of complication and challenge to those patterns you've already mastered because, for the first time, you and your horse are in motion as you ask him for frequent changes of direction, flexion, bend, and balance.

What This Pattern Does

■ **Improves your horse's balance, accuracy, and obedience.**
■ **Engages his attention and prevents the kind of boredom and disobedience that so often develops when he's just plunking around on the rail.**
■ **Increases his suppleness.** As he bends, the muscles on the outside of his curved body stretch, while the muscles on the inside relax. When he changes from one loop to another, his inside and outside switch. The muscles that were relaxed now stretch, and the muscles that were stretched now relax.

This is suppling at its best, and it's one reason you see even Grand Prix riders ride serpentines in their warm-ups (and why it is perfectly acceptable and even desirable to ride this gymnastic pattern at the posting trot).

■ **Shows you by comparison which side of your horse is stiffer and less able to bend.** If I were standing in the arena teaching you, we could figure that out together, but I'm not there, so it's up to you to feel his stiffness and softness and experiment with making minor adjustments. For example, if your horse feels softer and more bendable to the left, try riding him a bit

straighter in that direction so you don't risk overbending him. If he's stiffer and more board-like to the right— perhaps you feel him leaning against your right leg and hanging on the right rein—try increasing his bend a little going that way.

■ **Prepares you and your horse to smoothly and confidently execute bend- and direction-changing dressage test movements:** change of rein across the diagonal; 10-meter half-circle and return to the track;

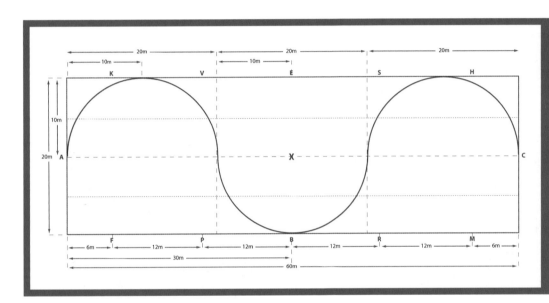

You can also school a serpentine in a 20-by-40-meter arena. Just ride two 20-meter half-circles that touch and change direction in the center. Note that with an even number of loops, you'll finish on the opposite hand.

Changing Bend, Balance, and Direction

1 On the first loop of the serpentine, Picasso and I have come off our 10-meter point on the rail and are headed toward a point on the centerline that's two meters beyond the letter V, so it's exactly 20 meters from A. To make sure we follow the circular track, I'm sitting deeper on my inside right seat bone. My inside right leg is at the girth, and I have Picasso flexed around my inside right rein. His chest is looking where he's going and his neck and head are coming straight out of his shoulders. My hips and shoulders are perpendicular to the track. I'm asking him to come around the turn by rhythmically pressing my outside leg against his side as I half-halt on my outside bearing rein.

2 As my body crosses the quarterline, I begin to prepare for the change of bend, balance, and direction. I soften the feel on my inside rein and even up the contact by taking a bit more feel on my outside rein. I relax my inside right leg at the girth as I start to bring my outside left leg forward to the girth. In response, Picasso relaxes the flexion in his jowl and begins to straighten through his body.

3 Approaching the centerline, Picasso's now in neutral: straight on the track from nose to tail. I'm in neutral too, with both my legs at the girth and equal contact on both reins. After I sit a bounce to pick up my new posting diagonal ...

4 ... I ask for a left flexion with my new inside left rein, sit deeper on my new inside left seat bone and bring my new outside right leg back. But I tell Picasso I want him to stay straight and not turn left yct with a fairly strong inside left leg.

5 At the moment my body crosses the centerline, I tell him it's now OK to curve onto the second loop of the serpentine. I relax the supporting pressure of my left leg at the girth and guide him around to the left with my outside right leg and rein. We'll touch the rail at B, and as I cross the next quarterline, I'll repeat this process going back the other way.

three-loop serpentine; turn right at B and left at E; leg-yield away from the rail and the mini-serpentine I call the "Figure S," where you change rein via a 10-meter half-circle left from E to X and a 10-meter half-circle right from X to B.

What You'll Do

You'll ride the serpentine the length of a standard 60-by-20-meter dressage arena at the trot. (You can adapt any arena set-up to this exercise, though.) Geometrically speaking, the three symmetrical 20-meter half-circles curve until they touch at the centerline. But anytime you change your horse's bend and balance, you have to do it gradually, and your horse has to have at least a moment between bends where he's "in neutral," in other words, straight.

The entire change from one bend to the other, therefore, should take about three strides. And those three strides should be accomplished before you reach the centerline, so you're completely ready to start the new half-circle going the other way.

Sound odd? It isn't really. It's just like having to be stationary at X and not three strides past X when you halt and salute, or back in working trot at H after lengthening stride across the diagonal, instead of halfway through the corner.

That means that you have to start preparing for the change of bend when your body, not your horse's nose or his tail, crosses the quarterline before the centerline. And those three strides between the quarterline and the centerline are going to be busy. You'll smoothly change the weight and balance in your seat, position, posting diagonal, and half-halting outside rein at the same time you change your horse's flexion, bend, balance, and direction.

What's more, even though you change his bend before the centerline, you still have to make sure he stays straight and doesn't dive off in the new direction. He must wait for your aids to say, "OK. Now we turn."

Flubs and Fixes

1 As I cross the centerline, I've clearly started turning to the left, but I haven't changed anything, not my legs, my seat, or Picasso's bend and balance. As a result he's a little counter flexed and falling in off the track on his new inside shoulder. This is going to make this new loop of the serpentine too small.

2 To correct Picasso's posture and get him back on track, I ask for a step of spiral-out. As I rise, I sit deeper on my inside left seat bone. I move my outside right leg back a bit. I take a firm enough feel of the inside left rein to say, "Hey, I want an inside flexion." And I press my left leg hard enough at the girth to tell Picasso to rebalance himself onto his outside right shoulder.

Tips for a Successful Serpentine

■ **Review.** Make sure you and your horse are comfortable and confident riding the gymnastic exercises leading up to this one, especially the 20-meter circle and the spiral-in and spiral-out. If you're struggling with them, put the serpentine on hold until you've made them better.

■ **Post the trot.** As with many previous exercises, posting will encourage your horse to go energetically forward, always the first requirement for quality in any exercise. And again, posting will help you with your timing. Every time you rise, you know that's the moment when you can influence your horse's inside hind and outside fore because they're in flight.

What's more, as I mentioned above, the serpentine is a terrific warm-up exercise, and you always post when warming up. Later, you should occasionally sit the trot because that's the way you'll be required to do the pattern in First Level Test 2.

■ **Know geometry.** (At least that of your dressage arena.) It's the best way to accurately find the points you have to touch on the rail and centerline. If you school in a 40-meter arena, you can still do the serpentine. Just ride two 20-meter half-circles and change the bend at X. If you're a hunter rider using a ring with a lot of jumps, just focus on the quality of the pattern. Ride to specific points even if they're not quite equidistant from each other and make sure your changes of bend are smooth and balanced.

■ **Challenge yourself.** As your horse gets stronger, suppler, and better trained, maximize the gymnasticizing effects of the serpentine by riding him forward with bigger strides and back with smaller ones within the pattern. Increase your accuracy and bend by riding four 15-meter loops or five 12-meter loops, but remember that to connect those half-circles, you'll have more straight strides across the centerline. When you ride an odd number of loops in the serpentine, by the way, you end up on the same hand. When you ride an even number, you finish on the opposite hand.

3 As I cross the centerline, I've given up my outside rein and crossed my inside left hand over Picasso's withers. This has overbent him so much that his haunches are swinging left and his shoulder is falling right. As a result, he's to the right of the track and the new loop of the serpentine is going to be big and odd-shaped.

4 I correct the problem with a step of spiral-in. I straighten Picasso's neck and head by softening on the inside left rein and taking a greater feel on the outside right rein. Then I ask him to bring his shoulders to the left by squeezing with my outside right leg a little behind the girth and applying a bit of a bearing outside right rein against his neck.

■ **Go both ways.** I'll talk you through one change of bend, from a right half-circle to a left half-circle as I'm doing in the photos on pages 64 and 65, but always do the pattern going both ways so you're switching as often from left to right to left as you are from right to left to right.

Ride the Serpentine

Pick up a posting trot to the right at A. Sit a bit deeper on your inside right seat bone with your inside right leg at the girth. With your inside right rein, softly flex your horse right at the jowl by turning the knuckles of your right hand toward your left hip.

> Ride some forward and back strides to reinforce the idea that when you squeeze, he's to go forward.

Keep your outside left leg a hair farther back than your inside right leg to encourage his poll-to-tail bend. And give just a little "maintenance" half-halt on your outside left rein by squeezing your left shoulder back and down every time you rise. Your horse should be on the bit, which means he's giving you a soft, conversational contact and is listening and responding.

Circle two or three times or until you're happy with your horse's balance, energy, and accuracy. The next time you come around to A, begin the serpentine by starting the first 20-meter half-circle just as if you were circling. From A, curve evenly around and touch the rail 10 meters from the corner. Then continue to curve around toward the centerline.

As your body crosses the quarterline, begin to prepare for the new bend. Start changing the flexion in your horse's jowl by first straightening him. Soften your inside right flexing rein and make the contact on both reins more even. As soon as he's straight and "in neutral," sit a bounce to change your posting diagonal from right to left.

As you do—and there are a lot of little things going on at this point—sit a bit more deeply on your new inside left seat bone. Move your new inside left leg forward, so it's on the girth. Move your new outside right leg a hair back so it's a bit farther back than your new inside leg. And softly ask for the new left flexion by turning the knuckles of your left hand toward your right hip.

This change can be quick, but it should also be smooth and seamless. I tell my students it's like passing a tennis ball from my right hand to my left. First I'm holding the ball only in my right hand, then for a split second I have both hands on it, and then it's only in my left hand.

Hold your horse's body with your new inside left leg so he continues straight until you cross the centerline (it should feel a little like spiraling-out). Then tell him it's OK to turn onto the new half-circle loop by softening the pressure of your inside left leg and increasing the pressure on your new outside right leg and rein, as if you're spiraling in. Ride the 20-meter half-circle to the left by touching the rail at B, and as you cross the quarterline, repeat the process of changing bend, balance, and direction, this time from left to right.

Finish the pattern at C, and then the decision of what to do next is up to you. If you weren't entirely satisfied with how the serpentine went, you can immediately segue right into another one at C. If it felt pretty good, ride into the corner to M, cross the diagonal to K, and begin a new left/right/left serpentine at A.

What If ...

■ Your horse falls in on the serpentine pattern and makes the new half-circle too small so you don't get to your next point on the rail? I guarantee when he changed his flexion and bend from right to left, he never changed the balance in his shoulders from his old outside left to his new outside right. Fix the problem by picking him up and out with a step of spiral-out to the right as soon as you change your seat and aids. Nobody will detect it, and your horse will once again be properly balanced.

■ You realize you're not going to hit your point because your circle is getting too big? Ask for a stride of spiral-in and boom! You're right on track again. That's what I love about spiral-in and spiral-out. It's much smoother—to say nothing of being more effective—than yanking on the reins and trying to pull him around.

■ Your horse loses impulsion, slows down, or comes above the bit when you ask him to change flexion and bend from right to left? Forget about the serpentine and ride two or three 20-meter circles to the right to restore the quality of the gait and the soft, conversational contact.

Ride some forward and back strides to reinforce the idea that when you squeeze, he's to go forward. Then, when you return to the serpentine, you've polished the tool that reminds him not to suck back and fall behind your leg. Also, firmly turn your inside knuckles toward your outside hip and half-halt on your outside rein to remind him that flexion around the inside rein means "stay on the bit, stay on the vertical, stay soft and listening."

CHAPTER 10

GYMNASTIC EXERCISE 10
LEG-YIELD TO/FROM THE RAIL

Teach your horse to move sideways as he's going forward.

The preparation for a correct leg-yield is a correctly ridden corner. I am riding Tim on a right turn with the correct bend, flexion, and balance. This will set him up for a proper leg-yield.

I N LEG-YIELD, YOUR HORSE keeps his body straight and parallel to the long side as he creates a diagonal track across the arena by crossing and passing his inside legs in front of and ahead of his outside legs. You'll begin working on this exercise by turning down the quarterline and moving away from the direction of his slight inside flexion toward the rail.

When that feels good, you'll increase the difficulty of the movement by coming through the corner onto the long side and changing the bend before you leg-yield toward the quarterline. (Note that no matter where your horse is in the arena relative to the rail, the "inside" of the movement is his concave or relaxed side; the "outside" is his convex or stretched side.)

Why Leg-Yield?
The leg-yield is a required dressage movement in First Level Tests 2, 3, and 4. For any English riding—not just dressage—it improves:

■ **Coordination.** You polish and refine the timing and balancing of your seat aids and half-halting rein aids. And

your horse gets better and more obedient about responding to them.

■ **Communication.** You start differentiating between forward- and sideways-driving seat aids. Here's how I do that: I imagine that beams of light are shooting out of my hipbones. When my horse and I are traveling straight ahead, I'm shooting those beams straight out on either side of him. Straight ahead is my direction of travel; straight ahead is the direction of the push in my seat. When I want to ask him to move sideways in a leg-yield, I very slightly change my seat so I'm sending the beam from my inside hip shooting toward his outside shoulder—the same forward-and-sideways line of travel I want his inside hind leg to take.

Leg-Yield to the Rail

1 I turn Tim off the short side onto the quarterline, maintaining his very energetic and expressive trot with my inside (right) leg at the girth. I ask him to turn with a squeeze of my outside (left) leg a hair behind my inside leg. I also have a bit of a bearing-rein contact with my outside rein and a soft flexing-rein contact with my inside rein. As a result, we're both "straight" on this gently curving line: He's evenly bent from poll to tail according to the track we're on, hind legs following forelegs; and my hips and shoulders are perpendicular to the track. I'm carrying my whip in my right hand so I'm prepared to tap or touch Tim on the inside to reinforce my inside leg aid if necessary.

2 We're on the quarterline, but I won't even think "leg-yield" until Tim's finished the turn and become as straight as I can get him. And look at this! He's so dead straight you can't even see his hind legs. But straight doesn't mean he's no longer got an "inside" and "outside." Even now I'm sitting deeper on my inside (right) seat bone, with my right leg at the girth and my outside (left) leg a bit farther back. He's slightly flexed to the inside, and I'm truly riding him from my inside leg to my outside rein. My right heel is probably off him a bit more than I would like, but it illustrates that you don't ride with your heel. You ride with the top of your calf and your knee, thigh, seat, and shoulder.

3 On the next up-beat, I start to ask Tim to leg-yield. I maintain a right flexion with my right rein. I turn my hips just enough that if a beam of light were coming out of my inside hipbone, it would be shooting toward his outside (left) shoulder. I bring my inside leg back so it's about even with my outside leg. I push forward and sideways to ask him to cross his inside hind in front of his outside hind, toward his left (outside) shoulder, and step ahead and left with his left fore. At the top of my post, I also half-halt on my outside rein to keep him from leaning on that shoulder and getting crooked.

- **Maneuverability.** Your horse's hindquarters become more supple and his shoulders get looser and freer.
- **Engagement.** By beginning to step forward and across with his hind legs, your horse starts bringing his hind end farther underneath him.
- **Connection.** Your horse develops a more elastic feel from his mouth to over his poll, down his neck, across his back, and into his haunches.
- **Cadence.** This is a subtle blend of balance, rhythm, and forward energy that enables him to move with expression, "air time," and pizzazz.
- **Lateral work.** Leg-yield lays a sturdy foundation for shoulder-in, travers (haunches-in), renvers (haunches-out), and half-pass.

OK, I hear you saying, "But Leslie, if my horse is moving forward-and-sideways in leg-yield, isn't he doing a lateral movement?" The practical answer is yes; the technical answer is no. Leg-yield is considered a "movement on

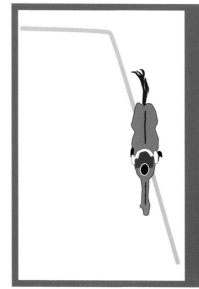

In the leg-yield the horse stays parallel to the rail with a slight inside flexion. The rider's inside leg is driving towards the rail while the horse's inside hind leg is coming up off the ground.

4 In the next stride—the down-beat, where I'm sitting—I soften and relax all my aids. Remember, applying your aids is like sending a message in Morse code: If the telegrapher held the key down all the time, it would send just one long beeeeeep; no message would get through. If I squeezed unrelentingly with my leg and rein, Tim would tune me out. Even though I'm relaxing my aids, however, my hips are still slightly turned and guiding him toward the rail.

5 And here, on the down-beat again, we arrive at the rail and I change my position, bringing my inside leg forward to the girth again and squaring up my hips so the diagonal push of my seat is now a straight-ahead push. (If those beams of light were coming out of my hips, they'd shine straight down the rail.) Tim, again, is dead straight on the rail.

Leg-Yield to the Centerline

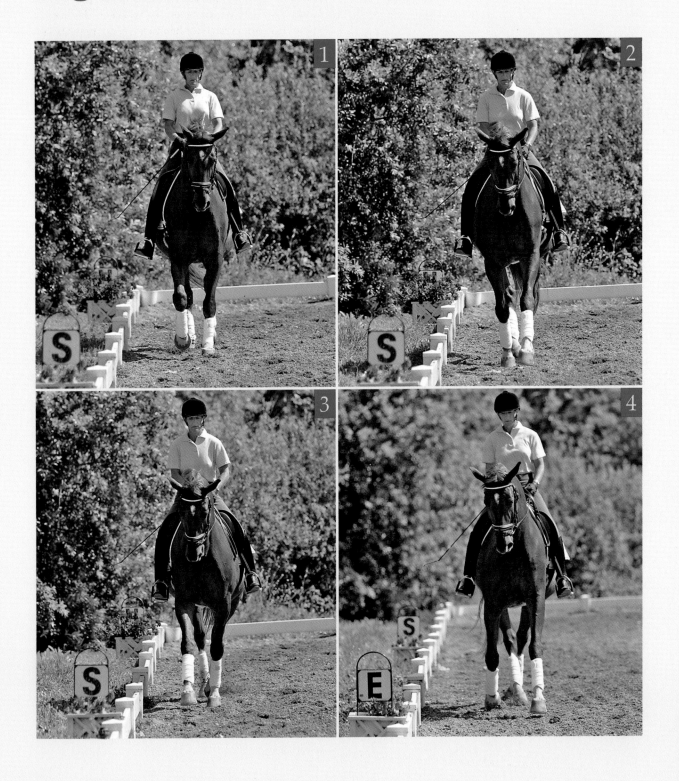

1 We've just come through the corner past H, and I'm riding one or two strides on the rail to make sure Tim is perfectly straight and correctly flexed to the inside (left). To leg-yield him away from the rail, I'm going to have to change his flexion and my position so his present "outside" becomes his "inside." Confusing? Just remember that inside and outside are always relative to your horse's bend and flexion.

2 I prepare to change everything from inside left to inside right by first putting Tim into "neutral." I relax my inside (left) rein so there's no flexion in his jaw. This is also the moment when I change my posting diagonal and bring my left leg back a bit from the girth so it's level with my new inside (right) leg, which I just leave slightly back where it is.

3 I've taken my time and a couple of strides to keep Tim straight on the rail even after establishing the new inside (right) flexion—because some horses just automatically fall to the outside as soon as you make the change.

4 But Tim has stayed straight and balanced and listening; so now, just as on the quarterline, I've begun my forward-and-sideways push—again, with my seat and not by digging my raised heel into him.

two tracks" because the horse's body stays straight from poll to tail, with his hind legs following in the step of his forelegs. For a movement to qualify as "lateral," his body has to bend just enough for him to travel on three tracks (shoulder-in) or four tracks (travers, renvers, and half-pass).

Leg-Yield Prerequisites

Make sure you're completely comfortable and confident with the gymnastic exercises leading up to this one, especially spiral-in/spiral-out (Chapter 8). In fact, I can almost guarantee that if you have the aids and timing to do a rhythmical, well-balanced, obedient spiral-out, leg-yield is going to be a piece of cake.

The other day I was giving a lesson to one of my young students and I said, "OK. Let me see a leg-yield." Well, suddenly this little girl turned into a pretzel, got all cockeyed, collapsed on one side, and started giving these funny aids. A leg-yield never happened. So I had her come back down to the C end of the arena and ride a gymnastic pattern she knew: spiral-in and spiral-out. As she finished the spiral-out and arrived back on the rail at C, I said "Now turn down the quarterline, travel straight for a few strides, then spiral-out to the rail." And her leg-yield was perfect!

Leg-Yield to the Rail

Tracking right, pick up a posting trot so you can time your aids. Remember, when you rise on the up-beat, your horse's inside hind and outside fore are starting to come off the ground—the only time you can influence his outside fore to hover and wait and his inside hind to step diagonally up underneath him. When you sit, you relax your aids.

Look where you're going. Position your inside leg at the girth and your outside leg a hair behind the girth. Keep your upper body tall, your shoulders square and perpendicular to the track, and your hips pushing out those beams of light on either side of his neck. Make sure he's giving you an energetic trot.

When you feel good, come through the short end of the arena. Ride past the first quarterline and the center-line, and turn down the second quarterline.

This is important: Getting to the rail by hook or by crook is NOT your goal. Your goal is to get there while your horse stays straight, balanced, and parallel to the long side. So before leg-yielding, trot on as far as you must to make sure he's straight from poll to tail, neither falling on his left shoulder nor pushing against your right leg.

His entire body should be beautifully balanced within the frame of your hands, legs, and light beams. If it's not, keep going—even if you have to ride the length of the arena on the quarterline, turn right when you reach the rail, and come all the way back around again. Believe me, not until he's energetic, straight, and balanced will the leg-yield happen.

Making sure you keep your horse's body pretty much parallel to the long side, with his left (outside) shoulder and left hip aligned, prepare to leg-yield: Ask for a soft inside flexion, so you can just see the arch above his right eye. Look ahead toward the rail at the end of the arena, where you want to end up, but don't start to twist or collapse just because you're going to go sideways. Keep your upper body perpendicular to the track and your shoulders tall and square.

With your heel down, bring your inside leg the teeniest bit back so it's even with your outside leg. As you rise, squeeze your outside (left) shoulder back and down to give your horse a little half-halt.

Sit and relax on the down-beat; as you rise again, push so the beams of light from your hip bones are now angled toward your horse's outside left shoulder. This angled push will encourage his inside hind to step diagonally forward and across. At the same time, half-halt on your outside (left) rein to keep his outside shoulder and hip lined up and to keep him from diving toward the rail.

> I'd much rather see you take the length of the arena to do a correct leg-yield than get to the rail in three crooked, hurried, unbalanced strides.

Maintain nothing more than a light, conversational feel on your inside (right) rein, enough to flex him at the jowl but not enough that his head and neck bend off to the right and no longer come straight out of the middle of his shoulders. This is a leg-yield, remember, not a rein-yield. If you pull his head and neck off to the right in an effort to make him go left, he'll fall on his left shoulder and end up crooked and falling to the rail. Every time you sit, relax your half-halting outside rein and the angled push in your seat. Every time you rise, activate them again.

You may have to go most of the way down the arena to get from the quarterline to the rail—not a big distance. But as long as your horse stays forward, straight, and obedient, that's more than OK. It's terrific! I'd much

rather see you take the length of the arena to do a correct leg-yield than get to the rail in three crooked, hurried, unbalanced strides.

Once you and your horse are pretty confident and correct doing this "shallow" leg-yield, start increasing the difficulty—but without sacrificing the quality—by making the angle steeper: perhaps reaching the rail two-thirds or half of the way down the arena. When you're pretty good at a steep angle, turn earlier—so that instead of leg-yielding across 5 meters, you're doing 6, 7, and eventually 10 meters from the centerline (as you're asked to do in First Level Test 2).

Leg-Yield From the Rail

Before I get to the how-to for this movement I want to explain its whys and wherefores. Most horses are naturally a bit stickier about leaving the magnetic pull of the rail, so you may have to be a bit stronger with the forward-and-sideways pushes in your seat. But otherwise your horse and rider position are going to be exactly the same as when you leg-yield from the quarter- or centerline.

The difference? Tracking right at the posting trot, you're going to come through the corner past A and toward K with a normal inside bend and flexion to the right. Within two or three strides after you pass K, you're going to prepare to leg-yield to the right by changing your position and your horse's bend and flexion from right to left. You made such a change for the three-loop serpentine in Chapter 9, and—just as then—he's going to have to stay straight through his body.

To set up this idea, invest some time in a "pre-exercise." Come through the corner tracking right at the posting trot, sitting a bit deeper on your inside (right) seat bone, with your inside leg at the girth and your outside (left) leg a hair farther back than your inside leg to encourage your horse's poll-to-tail bend. As you pass K, start changing the flexion in his jowl by softening your inside (right) flexing rein and making the feel on both reins even. As soon as he's straight, sit a bounce to change your posting diagonal from right to left. Sit a bit deeper on your new inside (left) seat bone, move your new inside leg forward so it's at the girth, and move your new outside (right) leg back a bit. Then softly ask for the new left flexion.

Now, with those beams of light from your hips and the pushes from your seat shooting straight up the rail, stay counter-bent all the way up the long side. When you

Wrongs

1 This is probably the most common mistake I see: I've turned into a pretzel. I'm twisting my upper body and collapsing and tilting so severely to the inside (right) that my hips and shoulders aren't even vaguely aligned. Tim responds to these confusing aids by continuing straight instead of leg-yielding.

2 The second most common mistake: I'm trying to ask him to leg-yield by pulling my right hand down and back, causing his nose and neck to overflex and bend right. Basically, I'm trying to "rein-yield" instead of leg-yield. Not only are my technique and position wrong, but I've so unbalanced Tim that he's falling left and shuffling instead of trotting with energy and expression, giving proof positive of another of my favorite rules: When a horse is unbalanced, he can't be in self-carriage.

get within three strides of H, repeat the process to change back to the right bend, again making sure your horse stays absolutely balanced and straight in the process. Come through the short side and repeat the exercise from M to F.

When you and your horse feel completely comfortable and confident with this exercise, come through the corner and leg-yield. As you pass K, take two or three strides to change bend, flexion, and posting diagonal. Then point those beams of light toward his outside (right) shoulder and leg-yield away from the rail. Again, you want to take it in baby steps, so aim for the quarterline 5 meters away. When you get to within three or four strides of the end of the arena, ride a straight stride or two; then change the flexion back to the right and turn right (believe me, a 5-meter turn to the left isn't going to happen).

As you and your horse get better, start going for a steeper track to the quarterline. Then gradually increase the distance until you can leg-yield to the centerline, where you have the choice of changing the flexion and turning right (as you have to do in First Level Test 3) or maintaining the bend and turning left.

What If ...

- **Confusion reigns.** Your horse seems confused or doesn't move away from your inside leg? First check that your aids are correct. If they are, remind him about moving away from your inside leg by walking, halting, and doing a little refresher course in turn on the forehand off your right leg. Or ride a spiral-in/spiral-out circle to the right at C; as soon as you've spiraled back out to the rail, ride past C, turn down the quarterline, get straight, and then just "spiral-out" to the rail.
- **The rail rules.** Your horse, feeling the magnetic pull of the rail, pops his shoulder, and leans so his haunches trail? First (and always), check your aids again. As I've said before, it's called a leg-yield, not a rein-yield. If you're trying to get him to move sideways by overbending him to the inside with the right rein, he's going to pop his outside shoulder, get crooked, and careen toward the rail.

Instead, soften your inside rein and teach him to

wait, listen, and stay straight with an exercise I call "Testing, one, two": Ride two leg-yield strides, then two straight strides, then two leg-yield strides all the way down the arena (remembering to switch your beams of light and your pushes back and forth). If you can do that, you know he's totally listening to you.

- **Your speed is zapped.** Your horse gets slower and slower and slower moving sideways? Give him a little extra kick, squeeze, or touch of the whip to get some "forward" back into his "sideways." If that doesn't work, don't hesitate to stop leg-yielding and ride straight forward until he's trotting energetically again.
- **The rush is on.** Your horse accelerates forward instead of moving sideways when you put your leg on? Check your aids: Make sure the pushes from your seat are diagonal, toward his outside shoulder, and not just straight ahead. And make sure you haven't come with too much leg. (I rate my aids on a scale of 1 to 10. Just riding straight around the arena, the "maintenance" push in my seat is probably about a 3. To ask for a leg-yield, my diagonal push is about a 3½ or at most a 4. So while it increases a little, it never goes from a 3 to an 8.)
- **Ailing alignment.** You can't feel whether your horse is straight? Ask a friend to watch you school. She can tell you if he's looking to the outside instead of the inside, he's too bent in the neck, or you're collapsing and leaning way too far to the inside to push him sideways.

Now that you can leg-yield, what should you do with it? Incorporate this useful exercise into your regular schooling session. When I warm up my horses at home—and of course, none of this is set in stone—I run through a regular thirty-minute routine of gymnastics.

I do some flexing of the jaw before I get on. I do spiral-in and spiral-out and forward and back. I do shallow and deep serpentines with two, three, four, and five loops. I do leg-yield (and more exercises that I'll be teaching you in upcoming chapters). After that, I school the individual movements I think each horse needs to work on.

This routine pays off when I get to a show because I do exactly the same warm-up. And when my horses know what I expect of them, they're confident, not confused or upset.

> Now that you can leg-yield, what should you do with it? Incorporate this useful exercise into your regular schooling session.

CHAPTER 11

GYMNASTIC EXERCISE 11:
LENGTHEN STRIDE AT THE TROT

Use this "flattened" figure eight to teach your horse to take longer steps while staying rhythmic and balanced.

In a correct lengthening, your horse moves forward out of a working trot, with longer steps and good thrusting hock action.

THE FIRST GYMNASTIC EXERCISE I TAUGHT you (see Chapter 1) was "forward and back." You began at the walk, using your seat (and by now you know that when I say "seat," I mean buttocks, seat bones, and thighs) to ask your horse to stretch his frame and take slightly longer strides, then compress his frame and take slightly shorter strides.

In doing so, you were starting to gymnasticize him by developing his longitudinal flexibility. You were also taking the first baby steps toward trot lengthening (a required movement at First Level), demonstrating that besides moving freely forward in a clear and steady rhythm while accepting contact with the bit, he'd begun to develop thrust, or pushing power, from behind.

With this exercise we're going to teach your horse how to do that lengthening. When we're finished, he'll responsively go more forward out of a working trot, with longer steps and good thrusting hock action, while his rhythm and balance stay the same and he maintains a steady light contact. And, just as important, he'll softly come back to working trot when you ask.

Why a Figure Eight?

Trot lengthenings in dressage tests appear on the diagonal, so most people assume that's where to teach them. But too often, unfortunately, when I ask a student to do a lengthening, I see her turn onto the diagonal line, put her body position in neutral, and start kicking with both legs and pulling with both hands. (Remember, even when you're on a perfectly straight line, you still have an inside driving leg and flexing rein and an outside holding leg and half-halting rein.)

Her horse, instead of taking longer, "thrustier" strides, either doesn't respond at all or grabs the bit, dives on his

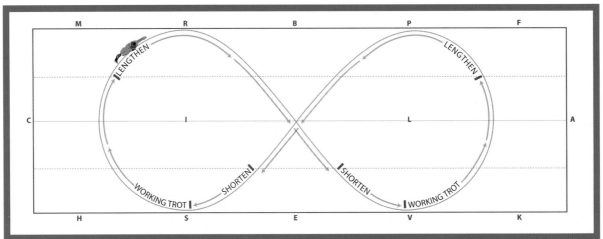

Your horse learns to go forward on the right hand by keeping his shoulder up and his haunches well under him, then in one smooth motion the rider changes to the left hand and maintains his engagement.

forehand and runs downhill, gets quick or irregular, breaks to canter, or takes a few lengthened strides and then fizzles because he doesn't have the strength or balance to carry himself any further.

I avoid these problems with the gymnastic pattern I call a "flattened figure eight" (see the diagram above). Unlike a true figure eight of two 20-meter circles, this one is made up of two 20-meter half-circles connected by straight diagonal lines. Tracking right, you'll start the first half-circle at S; after crossing the second quarterline before R, you'll start asking your horse to lengthen. You'll continue asking as you come off the rail and ride the straight three- or four-stride short diagonal over X. Then you'll start asking him to shorten back to working trot between the second quarterline and V, where you'll begin your second half-circle. As you cross the second quarterline before P, you'll start asking him to lengthen stride again.

Here's why this pattern works:

■ It reminds your horse that he knows the "feel" of lengthening. On the arc of each half-circle, his inside hind leg naturally steps more under him and carries, and his outside foreleg reaches, stretches, and travels farther than his inside foreleg.

■ It encourages you and your horse to change from a right flexion and bend to a left flexion and bend going across the short diagonal, just as you learned to do on the three-loop serpentine in Chapter 9. This change is key: As he goes from right to left, he has to lift and

change the balance in his shoulder; that lifting and rebalancing allow his hind legs to drive farther forward and make bigger strides. (Even though you ask for the lengthening before X, you'll feel a surge over X as he begins to get it. Eventually you'll feel him lift his shoulders and surge as soon as you put your leg on and ask for a lengthening.)

■ It limits the number of straight lengthening strides by putting them on a very short diagonal line, so your horse doesn't have the time or the distance to get confused, lose his balance, or fall apart. As he begins to understand and get stronger and more responsive, you'll move the 20-meter half-circles farther apart, gradually elongating the diagonal line. Soon you'll get to the ends of the ring and so reach your ultimate goal: lengthening across the full diagonal.

■ It gives your horse a clear, predictable pattern. Let's face it: Horses, being creatures of habit, do learn to anticipate. And although we normally don't want that, the truth is that a little bit of knowing what's coming and when can help when your horse is figuring out something new.

■ It shows you—by quick comparison—which hind leg is weaker. If, say, the right is weaker, on every half-circle to the right you'll feel less thrust from your horse's inside (right) hind, and you'll probably find you have more difficulty half-halting him up off his outside (left) rein. Carry your whip on that weaker side—there'll be too much going on to try to change it back and forth. And help him strengthen that leg by slightly modifying the pattern: Each time you go right, ride a circle and a half.

Now Ride the Pattern

Following the diagram on page 78, track right on a 20-meter circle that touches the rail at S and R and centers on the letter I. Post the trot to encourage your horse to go forward energetically, and to time your aids better: Squeeze with your driving inside (right) leg and half-halt with your outside (left) rein as you begin to rise; relax your aids as you sit.

Check your position: inside (driving) leg at the girth; outside (holding) leg a little bit back to help create a soft bend through your horse's body; inside (right) hand softly maintaining a right flexion in his jowl; outside (left) rein giving a soft "maintenance" half-halt as you squeeze your left shoulder back and down every time you rise.

Circle several times as you ask your horse to go just a very little bit forward and back, as you've done in the past. Without this obedient response, no matter how small, this pattern—which is nothing more than "forward and back" on a larger scale—will not work. When the circle feels good and he feels balanced and listening, begin the pattern: Touch the rail at S; cross the centerline; after crossing the quarterline before R, start encouraging him to lengthen his stride by driving more powerfully from behind. Every time you rise, push your seat strongly forward to ask him to step more powerfully under himself, and give a half-halt that asks him to lift his outside shoulder and "hover" it in the air.

> If, instead of coming back, your horse gets heavy in your hand and hangs, he's telling you he's lost the flexion and is pulling evenly on both sides of the bit.

Here's the key: To give your horse the time to lengthen his strides, you want to spend a bit more time pushing forward in the air as you rise, and a bit less time relaxing in the saddle as you sit. This will create a sense of suspension and hovering in his stride, instead of just letting him quicken or get irregular. Remember, your seat determines his length of stride, not the other way around. Resist the very strong temptation to follow your horse's rhythm and motion (his first response to your increased push will probably be to speed up); instead, focus on being the slow-and-steady metronome that gives him the time to lengthen his strides.

As you come off the rail at R, look toward V and begin to ride the short straight diagonal across X. Somewhere around X, change your horse's flexion and bend as you did on the three-loop serpentine, but a little less noticeably. We're looking for a subtle, almost invisible, change in your own position, and an equally subtle response from him: just enough to keep his inside shoulder and hip aligned and his jowl flexed to the inside. In truth, the only thing that should be visible to somebody watching is a really nice half-halt.

Soften your inside (right) flexing rein so the contact on both reins is more even and your horse is straight through his jowl. Sit a bounce to change your posting diagonal from right to left, and sit a bit deeper on your new inside (left) seat bone. Move your new inside (left) leg forward to the girth, and move your new outside (right) leg back just a hair. And softly ask for the new left flexion by turning the knuckles of your left hand toward your right hip. As you rise out of the saddle, continue to ask your horse to lengthen by pushing forward with your seat and half-halting on your new outside (right) rein.

Cross the quarterline. As you approach V, begin asking your horse to shorten back to a working trot again. Soften and shorten the push in your seat as you rise, and slightly increase your half-halt. (Don't stop pushing with your seat entirely. Even though you're asking him to shorten stride, you still want him to go forward.)

If, instead of coming back, your horse gets heavy in your hand and hangs, he's telling you he's lost the flexion and is pulling evenly on both sides of the bit. Restore the flexion by playing a little with your inside (left) rein. Also check that your reins haven't gotten too long. (The length of your reins determines the length of his frame; if they're too long, you'll never get him to shorten up.) Ride the rest of the half-circle in working trot; after crossing the quarterline before P, ask him to lengthen again.

After riding two diagonal lines (one going each way), walk and take a break. This is a very tough exercise, so both you and your horse are going to get winded and tired. Catch your breath; then come back and do it again. As the two of you get stronger, and your horse's lengthenings get better, work up to doing four consecutive diagonal lines. At that point, you can start to move your half-circles apart—until you're riding full diagonal lines from corner to corner. Repeat this pattern at least two times a week.

What If ...

■ **He's inconsistent.** Your horse comes off the bit or gets irregular or quickens? Keep pushing forward; don't shorten his stride or walk and try to reorganize. If you give up every time something runs amok, he'll quickly learn, "Hmmm. If I come off the bit or lose rhythm, I get to take a break and I don't have to go forward."

■ **He ignores you.** Your horse won't shorten and come back? Remember, one of the beauties of these gymnastics is that you can always step back and call upon a previous one. So get back on a 20-meter circle and school walk/trot, trot/walk, walk/trot until he's soft and listening. Or stay in the slightly lengthened trot but do some spiral-in and spiral-out to remind him that he also has to stay balanced and obedient.

■ **He leans on you.** You change the flexion and direction at X but your horse continues to lean to the inside and does not change his balance? A step or two of spiral-out will smoothly and imperceptibly get him to raise his shoulder and shift his balance to the outside.

The Flattened Figure Eight

1 As Cassiano and I come around the figure-eight pattern on the right half-circle in working trot, he's nicely flexed and bent to the inside from poll to tail. We've passed the quarterline before R, and here we're on the down beat, so I'm in the sitting phase of the posting trot and I've relaxed my aids.

2 In the next step, as I begin to rise on the up beat, I start asking Cassiano to lengthen his trot stride. I squeeze my left shoulder back and down to give a good half-halt that asks him to lift and "hover" his outside shoulder in the air, and I give a bigger, longer, stronger push with my seat (from my hip, down through my thigh, to just below my knee at a point that's about level with the bottom of my saddle pad). Note that my heel is not involved; in fact, I'm not even wearing spurs. Even so, he responds to my aids with a bigger, longer, more engaged step.

3 As I sit and relax again, Cassiano's still flexed to the right. But as I approach X and continue asking him to lengthen …

4 … I prepare to change the bend, flexion, and balance in his shoulders for the new half-circle to the left. First I soften the flexing contact on the inside (right) rein so he's momentarily straight in his jowl. I sit a bounce, and …

5 … in the next stride I sit deeper on my new inside (left) seat bone and flex him to the left, with his balance now on the right shoulder. He continues to step strongly forward from behind—and just look at the reach in his fore!

6 As we cross the quarterline before V, I lower and shorten my post and bring my shoulder blades together to ask Cassiano to come back and shorten his stride. Although this is probably more of a collected trot than a working trot, he responds smoothly and promptly. If he lengthens and comes back just as well in the other direction, we'll take a break, then move on to another exercise. One of the best ways to tell a horse he did a good job is to stop asking and either put him up or go on to something else.

CHAPTER 12

GYMNASTIC EXERCISE 12:
COUNTERBEND ON A SERPENTINE

Increase ridability by teaching your horse to bend his body one way while following a track that curves the other way.

Montero and I are performing turn on the forehand in half-pass position. He is moving his haunches into the direction of bend.

THIS IS ANOTHER OF MY FAVORITE gymnastic exercises. Why favorite? Because once you add it to your training toolbox, you're going to find that its gymnasti-cizing effect is almost magical.

The shape is the same basic serpentine I taught you back in Chapter 9: three 20-meter half-circles that touch and change direction at the centerline. But where, for that figure, you changed your posting diagonal, your own position and aids, your horse's bend and flexion, and the balance in his shoulder as you went across the centerline, for this one you'll keep them the same.

This means that as you go around the middle loop, he'll be "counterbent": The flexion in his jowl, the even bend through his body from poll to tail, and the direction in which he's looking will all be to the outside of the track. (Remember, though, that no matter where he is relative to the figure, track, or rail, the "inside" of the movement or exercise is his concave or relaxed side and the "outside" is his convex or stretched side.) Your seat and upper body, which will remain perpendicular to the track, will tell him where he's to go; your outside leg, and the way you squeeze and drive with it, will tell him how to position and hold his body.

This exercise not only improves your horse's accuracy and obedience; it engages his attention, increases his suppleness, and …

■ Logically and doably introduces the feel and idea of counterbending. Rather than asking for a counterbend out of the blue, you'll establish his "true bend" position and shape on the first loop, then simply allow it to stay the same on the second loop.

■ Teaches him to move away from your outside driving leg and into the direction of his flexion and bend by passing and crossing his outside legs in front of his inside legs. He'll need to know how to do this for counter-canter work (where, on a circle to the right, say, he can-

ters on the left lead) and for the three- and four-track lateral movements of travers or haunches-in, renvers or haunches-out, and half-pass, a dramatic and expressive movement where the horse stays basically parallel to the rail as he follows a diagonal line while bending and looking in the direction that he's moving.

■ Increases your body awareness and his balance and maneuverability. That's important because any horse, but especially a dressage horse, should be so supple and obedient that he can go anywhere in the arena at any time and in any body position. And that's why I introduce counterbending before shoulder-in (which comes first in most trainers' programs and even in the dressage tests).

■ Tips you off (once again) to your horse's stiffer side—he'll be less able to counterbend going that way—and gives you a ready-made tool for helping him to bend more evenly.

■ Supplements your posting-trot warm-up. I do this serpentine at least once in each direction, on every one of my horses, every time I ride at home or at a show. And,

Problem Solving

If you just can't push your horse's haunches over as you begin the counterbent loop of the serpentine, or if you feel as if you're going to run into the rail because he's baffled by what you're asking, quietly ask him to halt. Go back and make sure he understands your aids and the response you want by asking for a turn on the forehand in half-pass position. If that feels good, walk off, pick up the trot, and then come and try the serpentine again.

I'm also going to suggest something you probably never thought you'd hear from me: Your trot may be too energetic and forward to let you control his position and steps. Slow things down by riding the serpentine at the walk or easing off on the trot a little (but continue to keep him in front of your leg).

You can also make the track less difficult by riding a shallow serpentine between the rail and the centerline (see diagram, page 86): Start at C, touch the rail 10 meters from the corner, come off the rail heading toward X, change your aids as you cross the quarterline, touch X, change your aids as you cross the quarterline, touch the rail 10 meters from the corner, and finish at A.

Remember, you can always go back a notch and make sure your horse really understands the exercises that lay the groundwork for this one, or make this pattern as simple as you possibly can (so you're still asking, but in a way that he can understand and answer). Going back or doing a "baby version" doesn't mean you're losing a battle and you're going to get stuck there. It means you're avoiding a fight—and fighting never teaches a horse anything. Two or three weeks down the road, you're suddenly going to realize that he gets it, or that his muscles have sufficiently built up to do the job.

magically, it makes them more ridable. They seem to develop more "gears." And their steering seems to become power steering.

Before You Start

Prepare your horse for the idea of moving away from your outside driving leg and into the flexion and bend by going back to the halt and teaching him to do a turn on the forehand in half-pass position. I like to begin this way because, just as with the regular turn on the forehand (Chapter 7), it establishes a low-key, low-stress atmosphere in which your horse is less likely to get confused or upset than if he were in motion.

You'll be better able to concentrate on the feel and timing of your aids. And if he just can't or won't figure out what you're asking, you can always have a helper stand next to him, put one hand on your outside calf and the other on his outside hip, and calmly, quietly reinforce your sideways-driving outside leg with a push.

Review the "turn on the forehand" chapter, then study and follow photos 1 and 2 at right for how-to instructions. Remember to hold your whip in your outside hand in case your horse needs an encouraging little tickle or tap to reinforce your leg. Sit deep on your inside seat bone, with your upper body tall and square and your outside leg a little bit back from your hip down to your heel.

As soon as your horse responds to a squeeze of your outside leg by moving his haunches one step around his forehand in the direction of his flexion and bend, relax your leg aid. Then squeeze again. When your horse is responding promptly, confidently, and reliably in both directions, check out Chapter 9's three-loop serpentine column. Then go ahead and …

Ride the Counterbend Serpentine

Tracking right at C, pick up a posting trot to keep your horse moving energetically forward and to help you time your aids. As I've told you before, the best moment to influence

(Continued on page 88)

Turn On The Forehand in Half-Pass Position

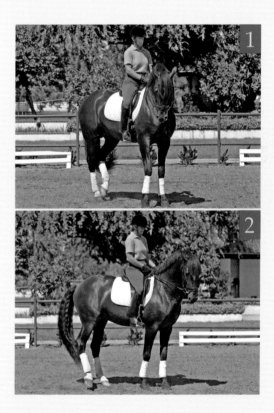

1 I prepare Montero for the counterbend serpentine by teaching him to respond to my driving outside-leg aid. From the halt he'll move his haunches around his forehand in the direction of his flexion and bend. At the halt, I turned my right knuckles toward my left hip, asking him to flex his jowl to the right a little more than usual. Sitting on my right seat bone, I squeeze behind the girth with my left leg to ask him to step his left hind across and in front of his right hind.

2 The movement ends when Montero lifts, moves and sets down his right leg. Again, I have a bit more flexion than usual (although his neck is still coming straight out of his shoulders) because I never want him to confuse turn on the forehand with another movement done from the halt: reinback.

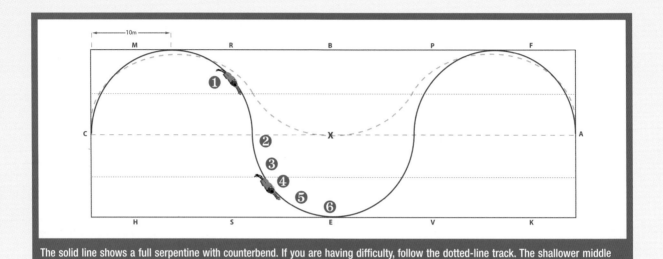

The solid line shows a full serpentine with counterbend. If you are having difficulty, follow the dotted-line track. The shallower middle loop makes the exercise less difficult. (The numbers on the diagram correspond to the photos below and at right.)

Three-Loop Serpentine With No Change of Bend

1 Tracking right at the posting trot, we've touched the arena rail on the first 20-meter loop of the three-loop serpentine and are headed toward the centerline. Montero is moving energetically forward off my inside (right) driving leg. He's slightly flexed to the right in his jowl and has an even bend through his body, from poll to tail. I'm sitting deep on my inside seat bone, my seat and shoulders perpendicular to the circular track.

2 Crossing the centerline I'm still sitting on my inside seat bone and Montero is still flexed to the right. I've taken a little more indirect inside rein—without crossing my hand over the withers—to create just a bit more flexion in his jowl than on the first half-circle. I slide my whole outside (left) leg back, hip to heel. As I sit on the down beat, I give a sideways squeeze (exactly as I did in the turn on the forehand in half-pass position) to ask him to cross and pass his outside (left) hind leg in front of his inside hind and keep his haunches right. Even though we're starting to follow the 20-meter half-circle track around to the left on the serpentine, he's counterbent around my inside (right) leg, his inside hip following his inside shoulder.

3 Although there's still a bit more flexion in Montero's jowl, his neck is coming straight out of his shoulder and the front of his chest is looking where he's going. Again, his inside (right) hip is nicely following the path of his inside shoulder. Me? While my outside leg is telling him what to do, my position is telling him where to go to do it: My shoulders and hips are perpendicular to the left-curving track, and my inside (right) hipbone is clearly pointing toward E.

4 As we cross the quarterline on the down beat, I sit and squeeze with my outside (left) leg—and Montero very expressively steps so far under and across with his outside hind that it almost lines up with his inside fore; both of them are pointing directly at E. He still has a nice but not overdone flexion to the inside; my position is still telling him exactly where we're going.

5 In the next stride, I start to rise on the up beat and relax my outside (left) leg aid, but Montero continues to come forward toward E, his inside hip following his inside shoulder and a nice bend from the tip of his ears to the top of his tail. He's definitely out in front of my leg and marching forward.

6 And his haunches have stayed to the inside (right) and followed the 20-meter half-circle track so well that his inside hind has just touched the rail at E. We'll keep everything exactly the same until we approach the centerline, where I'll relax my indirect inside rein, bring my outside leg forward, start squeezing and driving on the up beat with my inside (right) leg, and turn my seat and shoulders so they're perpendicular to the right-curving track. After A, I'll come through the corner and across the diagonal, then start the same pattern on the left hand.

your horse's inside (right) hind with a driving push of your inside leg and seat and influence his outside (left) fore with a half-halt on your outside rein is when those feet are starting to lift into the air and come forward.

But to counterbend on the middle loop of the serpentine, you're going to use your outside (left) leg to tell his outside (left) hind to step across and inward. Because his inside flexion and bend—and so your posting diagonal—stay the same throughout the pattern, you'll squeeze with your outside (left) leg as you begin to sit, because that's when his outside hind is coming off the ground. And you'll relax that leg as you begin to rise, because his outside hind will be on the ground.

As you circle, check your aids and position. Sit a

> Once your horse reliably and comfortably does the three-loop serpentine with no change of bend in both directions, start increasing its gymnasticizing effect. Turn the counterbent middle half-circle into a circle-and-a-half.

bit deeper on your inside (right) seat bone, with your inside leg at the girth. Softly flex your horse at the jowl with your inside rein by turning the knuckles of your right hand toward your left hip. Keep your outside (left) leg a hair farther back than your inside leg to encourage his poll-to-tail bend. And every time you start to rise, give a little "maintenance" half-halt on your outside rein by squeezing your left shoulder back and down, making sure that he's on the bit—that he's giving you a soft, conversational contact and is listening and responding.

When you're happy with your horse's balance, energy, and accuracy, begin the first 20-meter half-circle at C. Touch the rail 10 meters from the corner; then smoothly continue around on the right hand toward the centerline. As you approach the centerline, soften the driving push of your right leg and seat but continue to stay deep on your inside (right) seat bone. (If you shift your weight to your outside seat bone in an effort to push his haunches over, you'll put too much weight on his right shoulder—and it is an absolute requirement that when he is flexed to the right, he is balanced onto his left shoulder.)

Slightly flex your right wrist to create a little more flexion in your horse's inside (right) jowl without bend-

ing his neck, which should still come straight out of the middle of his shoulders. Bring your outside (left) leg slightly farther back, but keep it long and deep and don't raise your heel. Tell your horse where you want him to go by keeping your own riding position perpendicular to the new left-curving track, with your eyes, shoulders, chest, and right hipbone looking toward the letter E.

Each time you sit, squeeze and push with your left leg to tell him to move his haunches to the right by crossing and passing his left hind leg in front of his right hind. The feeling you're after: His haunches are going toward the rail and his inside (right) hip is following the track of his inside shoulder.

As you continue around the left loop, just maintain your position. Keep the slightly increased flexion to the inside right. Keep a little stronger, more powerful outside (left) leg. Stay deep on your inside seat bone. Keep drawing the pattern by looking around the track with your eyes, shoulders, chest, and seat.

Touch the rail at E. As you continue around and approach the centerline, prepare to go back onto the third loop by beginning to change your aids: Slightly lessen the inside (right) flexion. Relax the inward-driving push in your left leg and slide it slightly forward, but still keep it a bit behind your right leg. As you do this, increase the driving push of that right leg … and BOOM! You're back on the right half-circle, with a true bend and flexion to the right. Continue to A, come through the corner, change rein across the diagonal, and at C start riding the serpentine curving around to the left this time.

Kick It Up a Notch

Once your horse reliably and comfortably does the three-loop serpentine with no change of bend in both directions, start increasing its gymnasticizing effect. Turn the counterbent middle half-circle into a circle-and-a-half. Or come around, touch the rail at E, ride straight down the long side for two or three strides counterbent in the renvers or haunches-out position, and then ride the last loop (which will just be a bit smaller). Or, more challenging still, combine some of my favorite patterns by riding a 20-meter counterbent circle as you go forward and back or spiral in and out.

CHAPTER 13

GYMNASTIC EXERCISE 13:
TWO TRACKS ON A CIRCLE

Improve straightness by teaching your horse to move his haunches to the inside.

I am asking Picasso to walk in a small half-circle with his shoulders on the 10-meter arc and his haunches on the nine-meter arc.

IN THE LAST EXERCISE YOU WORKED to increase your horse's ridability by teaching him to "counterbend," meaning to curve his body one way while following a track that curved the other way. To do this he developed a new skill: moving away from your outside driving leg and into the direction of his flexion and bend.

In this exercise we'll take that skill a step further. At the walk on a 10-meter circle, your horse will again stay flexed and bent in the direction of travel—but while his forehand follows the track of the 10-meter circle, he'll respond to your outside driving leg by gradually moving his haunches in about 1 meter, or a horse's width, to what we call "the second track." After a few steps in this position you'll gradually allow him to move his haunches back out to the 10-meter track again.

I specifically use this gymnastic to prepare my horses for turn on the haunches, a movement that first appears at Second Level, and for walk and canter pirouettes, which first appear at Fourth Level. In turn on the

haunches, a horse maintains even, quiet, regular steps as his forehand walks a circle around his haunches. In a pirouette, for which his gait must be collected, the radius of the circle he traces around his haunches must be no greater than the length of his body. These movements may be done through quarter, half, or full turns.

Although at Grand Prix the tests no longer call for walk pirouettes, even my Grand Prix horse Cassiano does the exercise I'll show you here. Why? Because it's really all about fine-tuning and gymnasticizing, and that's something that never stops. So even if you never plan to ride a dressage test, this gymnastic will supple and strengthen your horse and increase his obedience and maneuverability. Here's how:

■ It encourages him to step his haunches up underneath him. (A jumper can't make a very sharp rollback turn if his hind end is out behind him and falling to the outside.)

■ It teaches him to recognize and respond to subtle changes in your seat and aids as you ask him to go from straight to two-track to straight again. (Remember, when I say "straight," I mean aligned poll-to-tail according to the track he's on, with his haunches following his

forehand and his inside hip correctly lined up with his inside shoulder.)

■ It increases your feel for and control over his hind end, which helps you feel for and improve his straightness (every horse naturally tends to carry his haunches a bit right or left).

Because I teach this pattern before I introduce shoulder-in and haunches-in, my sequence may seem a bit "cattywhompus" to some. But this exercise is done at the walk so everything's a bit slower and more controllable; you can focus on your aids, how they feel, and how your horse is responding to them. What's more, until you can maneuver, position, and control his hind end, you don't have a chance of getting the engagement, power, and suspension you'll need for a lateral movement such as shoulder-in.

Prerequisites

You're starting to create the picture of a truly gymnasticized horse—but now, more than ever, all the individual little gymnastic dots really have to connect. Make sure that you and your horse are comfortable and confident doing each exercise in the series, but with special emphasis on forward and back at the walk, spiral-in and spiral-out, turn on the forehand in leg-yield and half-pass position, and three-loop serpentine with no change of bend.

Check your all-important timing. I've said it a hundred times, but it bears repeating: An aid can be effective only if it's given as the leg you're trying to influence lifts off the ground and begins its flight forward. As I talk you through this gymnastic you're going to be tracking right, so the leg you'll want to influence is the left—the outside—hind.

Because a walk stride consists of four consecutive steps—left hind, left fore, right hind, right fore—you can figure out when to activate and move the left hind by glancing down and checking your horse's right shoulder (it swings forward immediately before his left hind does), feeling the movement of his rib cage (it swings against your right leg when his left hind is in motion), or feeling his back (it drops a bit on the left when his left hind comes forward). The moment you feel this is when you squeeze.

Finally, get a response! If you put your leg back to ask your horse to move his haunches in, and three or four strides later they still haven't moved, you're not being a good teacher. Carry your whip on the outside; if he doesn't at least start to move off your leg aid, tickle or tap him behind your left leg (timing your tickle or tap

Two Tracks on a Circle

Aids checklist:

■ Walk on a 10-meter circle, right.

■ Sit deeper on right seatbone.

■ Keep hips and shoulders perpendicular to track.

■ Keep right leg at girth.

■ Keep left leg slightly behind right.

■ Turn knuckles of right hand toward left hip to flex his jowl.

■ Squeeze left shoulder back and down (half-halt) when his left shoulder comes up.

■ Make sure he's responsive to your leg (ride forward-back; spiral-in, out).

■ Turn knuckles of right hand toward left hip even more for greater flexion.

■ At same time, bring left leg back; turn right hip toward his left ear.

■ Press with left leg as his left hind lifts off the ground so he steps farther under himself toward his right shoulder.*

■ In next step, half-halt on left rein, bringing left wrist a bit toward right to encourage his outside fore to come in.

■ The motion will push right seat bone forward, which helps maintain his energy.

■ After three/four steps, relax aids and walk full circle to refresh his energy.

■ Try again.

How to tell when your horse's left hind is lifting off ground:

■ His right shoulder swings forward just before his left hind does.

■ His rib cage will swing against your right leg when his left hind is in motion.

■ His back will drop on the left when his left hind comes forward.

just as you would a leg aid: when his outside hind is lifting up off the ground and starting to come forward).

Be firm and clear, but be patient. Your horse will probably make a lot of mistakes while he's learning this exercise. He may lean on his inside shoulder. He may swing his haunches waaaaay to the inside. It may be a little messy, but hey! It's messy when you feed a child his first solid food. His execution might not be the best, but at least he's telling you, "I'm trying." First, get his willingness to respond; each time you try after that, you can look for a bit more perfection.

Two Tracks on a Circle

Pick up an energetic, marching walk to the right on about a 10-meter circle. Make sure your horse is "straight" on the circle—so that if you were to draw an imaginary 10-meter circular line in the air, his inside hip and shoulder would both be touching that line. Carry your whip on the outside, where it's ready to give him a tickle or tap to reinforce your outside (left) leg aid.

Sit a bit deeper on your inside (right) seat bone, with your hips and shoulders perpendicular to the track. Keep your inside (right) leg—your gas pedal—at the girth and your outside (left) leg, from your hip down to your heel, slightly behind the inside leg and just there, supporting. By now he should know how to walk a 10-meter circle; but if he happens to fall or drift out, your left leg will be ready to correct him with a step or two of spiral-in.

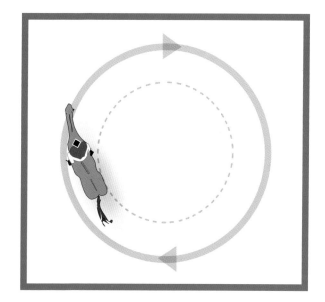

Make sure his chest is perpendicular to the track and his neck is coming straight out of the middle of his withers as you turn the knuckles of your right hand toward your outside (left) hip to flex his jowl just enough to let you see the corner of his right eye. Every time his outside shoulder comes up, squeeze your left shoulder back and down to give him a little "maintenance" half-halt on the next foot to lift, his inside hind.

Do some forward and back. Do a little spiral-in to an

Outside Aids

This is what is happening on the outside a moment before photo 2 on the next page:

As Picasso's outside hind starts to come off the ground, I give a driving squeeze to tell it to move across and ahead to the inside. I'm not using a spur to get the job done, and I'm not using just my heel. Yes, my heel has risen a bit because I've brought my leg back, but my aid is my whole leg, from my seat through my thigh down to my upper calf just below my knee.

8-meter circle, then spiral back out to a 10-meter circle. Check that your "go button" is working by having him lengthen and shorten stride in response to your seat. You can even leave the circle and do some turn on the forehand and three-loop serpentine with no change of bend. Until you're sure he's alert, responsive, and out in front of your seat and leg, the exercise will NOT work.

Once you feel your horse is tuned up and ready, ask him to move his haunches in to the second track. Use a bit more indirect inside rein: without crossing over the withers, turn the knuckles of your right hand even more toward your left hip to produce an ever-so-slightly greater flexion to the inside. At the same time, bring your outside leg back from the hip and slightly turn your pelvis to the outside. If a laser beam were shooting out of your inside (right) hip bone, it would be shining on his outside (left) ear.

Now that you're sitting in the correct, most effective position, press with your outside leg as your horse's outside hind lifts off the ground. He should step farther underneath himself in the direction of his inside shoulder. On the next step, give a little half-halt on your outside rein to encourage his outside fore to cross in a tiny little bit so his forehand stays on the 10-meter track. (Ordinarily, your half-halt comes straight back in your outside shoulder all the way down through your wrist. For this half-halt, though, bring your wrist a bit toward the inside to encourage his outside fore to come in.)

But you don't drive with just your outside hip, seat, and thigh. When I use my outside leg, it almost feels as if that motion pushes my inside seat forward, which maintains my horse's forward energy. Yes, my outside leg has become more active, and the driving

Two Tracks on a Circle

1 I make sure that Picasso is walking energetically on a 10-meter circle. I'm sitting a bit deeper on my inside seat bone, with my hips and shoulders perpendicular to the track; if my hip bones were emitting laser beams, they'd be shooting straight past either side of Picasso's ears. My inside leg is at the girth, rhythmically driving him forward, and my outside leg is a hair behind my inside leg, just there on his flank, supporting him. He has a nice little flexion to the right in his jowl, and he looks relaxed but alert as we maintain a soft but even feel on both reins. I'm carrying my whip in my left hand so I can immediately give a tap to reinforce my outside leg aid.

2 By turning my inside (right) knuckles more toward my outside (left) hip, I create a bit more flexion to the inside without bending Picasso's neck or turning his forehand off the track. I've brought my outside leg back from my hip down to my heel, which has automatically turned my seat just enough that my inside hip bone is pointing toward his outside ear. In response to my outside leg aid, he really stepped under and across with his outside hind. Now, in the next step, he's responding to the inward half-halt on my left rein by crossing his left fore a little bit. This will keep his forehand on the 10-meter track.

force on the inside is maybe a bit less, but I don't give it up altogether. Instead, I drive the outside hind under and across; then I drive the inside hind forward. There's a very subtle "left, right, left, right" rhythm and feel to it.

This is important: The only thing in this exercise that changes is the position of your horse's haunches. Everything else—pace, rhythm, contact—stays the same. He must march forward and stay out in front of your leg, soft in the contact, and supple in his jaw.

After three or four steps with your horse's haunches on the second track, soften your indirect inside flexing rein. Stop driving with your outside leg and bring it forward again. Straighten your pelvis so it's perpendicular to the track (those laser beams shooting out of your hip bones are shining straight out on either side of his head).

Walk at least a full circle around to refresh his energy, rhythm, and contact. Then try again.

When your horse responds smoothly, promptly, and correctly for three or four steps of two-tracking, gradually start to increase to five, six, seven, and eight—but never do more than ten, which would be almost half a circle. The idea is not for him to maintain the position as much as it is to understand your aids and respond promptly to them.

What if ...

- **Snail trail.** Your horse slows down and starts creeping like a snail? Immediately get straight on the circular track and make him go forward. The Number 1 quality you need to make this—and any—gymnastic work is forward energy.
- **Confusion sets in.** Your horse acts confused or

3 My outside leg aid automatically pushed my inside seat bone deeper and a bit more forward, and Picasso is responding to this aid by stepping his inside hind up and under. My outside leg is quiet at this point, but he's keeping his haunches in because of the slight rotation in my shoulder and my pelvis.

4 Once again I've come back to my outside driving leg to continue asking Picasso to bring his haunches to the inside—and at this moment I'm again asking him to bring his outside fore a little bit around so he stays on the 10-meter track. His chest is still looking directly where he's going, and his neck couldn't be straighter coming out of his shoulders. I don't have a whole lot of flexion, but at this point it's OK.

→

5 And here we are at about the ideal maximum position for this gymnastic, with Picasso's forehand on the 10-meter track and his haunches in on the second track, about a horse's width to the inside. A visual clue that this position is about right: The spaces between his legs are just about equal. Once again, we're at the moment where my inside hip has just pushed forward and engaged his inside hind. Even though this is the maximum position I'd ask, my aids aren't any stronger or more obvious. I'm still sitting upright in the saddle, not leaning or tilting to the outside. As long as he maintains an energetic, forward walk, we'll continue like this for three or four strides. Then …

6 … I start allowing him to straighten. I slightly soften the flexion to the right and return my pelvis and shoulders to neutral. (I'm still sitting deeper on my inside seat bone.) Instead of bringing his outside fore a bit to the inside, he's stepped straight ahead.

7 And here we are back on the 10-meter circle, with Picasso's inside hip definitely following his inside shoulder. (He looks a little haunches-in because of the photo angle, but he's evenly bent from poll to tail and his feet are stepping on the same track.)

doesn't understand? Clarify what you're asking by going back and doing turn on the forehand in half-pass position.

■ **A lingering lean.** Your horse leans on his inside shoulder and turns his chest so it's looking out instead of around the track toward where he's going? The most common cause of this problem is rider position, so check that you're not leaning to the outside and trying to use your upper body to push his haunches inward. Sit up, sit a bit deeper on your inside seat bone, and ask for a tiny bit more inside flexion by playing with your indirect inside rein. If the normal amount of flexion is a 10, ask for an 11 or 12 until he shifts his weight back onto his outside shoulder.

■ **He's one-sided.** You discover that your horse has an easy way and a hard way? The easy way is almost going to be too easy; it's there, and he'll just give it to

you. But you can't just say, "Oh, this is fun. Let's keep doing this." Not only do you have to go back to the hard way; you have to spend twice as much time working that side.

Make It Even MORE Gymnastic

By now you know that when you combine these exercises and make them more difficult, you increase their power. So put this one on a bigger circle and do it at the trot. With your horse's haunches in on the second track, do walk/trot/walk transitions. Go forward and back, or do spiral-in and out (but note that spiraling-out while he's holding his haunches in is very difficult). Soon enough, if and when you want to take on walk pirouettes, you will have such total control over your horse that you can just move him around any way you want.

CHAPTER 14

GYMNASTIC EXERCISE 14:
COUNTER-CANTER IN FIVE STEPS

It DOESN'T have to be a big deal! Here's how to make this

movement into just another gymnasticizing exercise.

This is the essence of counter-canter—even though I'm asking Picasso to canter on the left lead while he follows a curving track to the right, we're maintaining the rhythm, bend, balance, seat, and aids of a true canter.

THE COUNTER-CANTER—IN WHICH YOU deliberately keep your horse cantering on the left lead, say, while he follows a track that curves to the right—seems to cause panic in an awful lot of riders. And that's a shame because it's a useful (and in some cases required) skill that's really not hard to master.

If you do equitation or dressage, you need counter-canter for competition: In equitation, it's one of the tests a judge may ask you to do. In dressage, it first appears as a shallow serpentine at First Level; by the time you get to Fourth Level, you're asked to counter-canter through the corner onto the short side.

But even if you never want to show, counter-canter is a terrific addition to your training toolbox. By asking your horse to canter on a bending track to the right, say, while he maintains his lead, flexion, and bend to the left, counter-canter develops these important qualities:

■ **Suppleness:** He becomes more flexible when the

flexion in his jowl and the direction in which he's looking are to the outside of the track. These, of course, directly relate to the even bend through his body from poll to tail. (Remember that wherever he is relative to the rail or track, the "inside" is his flexed, concave, or relaxed side, and the "outside" is his convex or stretched side.)

■ **Balance:** When he can keep his haunches behind his shoulders no matter what track he's on, he improves his overall equilibrium.

■ **Engagement:** By requiring him to step deeper under his body, counter-canter encourages him to sit down more and elevate his forehand.

■ **Teamwork:** You're teaching him to disregard external circumstances ("But we're going the wrong way!") and submit unquestioningly to the control of your seat and aids. And that's important. As I've said before, any horse—but especially a dressage horse—should be so obedient that he smoothly and willingly goes anywhere in the

STEP 1:
The "Paper Clip"

On the left lead, I'm sitting perfectly perpendicu-lar to a long angled track from H toward A (see diagram at right). Harmony's Picasso—who, at the 2005 California Dressage Society's Championship show, was named CDS Open Fourth Level Horse of the Year and Great American/US Dressage Federation Open Fourth Level Region 7 Champion!—has his haunches following his shoulders, his inside left hip directly behind his inside shoulder. I have just a little extra inside flexion—perhaps because I feel him thinking about a flying change—but he's still well within the realm of what's correct. His nose is just a hair past the center of his chest, and he's balanced, supple, soft, and listening.

arena, on any track, at any time, and in any body position. (All my upper-level horses can comfortably counter-canter a volte—a circle that's 6 or 8 meters in diameter.)

Counter-Canter ISN'T a Big Deal

… but, unfortunately, you can make it a big deal by not properly preparing your horse to do it. I can't tell you how often it's happened that I ask a new student to show me a little counter-canter and she immediately puts her horse on a 20-meter circle or tries to counter-canter around the short side of the arena. Because she's asked for too much too soon, he loses his balance, grabs the bit, gets stiff, breaks to trot, or tries to do a lead change. Worse, you can really make it a big deal if, when you ask for counter-canter, you change your riding or your horse's way of going. I don't know why, but as soon as I say the words "counter-canter," students seem to think

they have to twist, tip, wiggle, or tilt while they let their horses slow down, speed up, lean, or change the balance in their shoulders.

That's why I use a five-step method that clearly, logically, and systematically introduces the skills and concepts of counter-canter. Follow these steps and eventually, regardless of the figure you're riding, you'll counter-canter the same way you canter: correctly main-taining the same rhythm, bend, balance, seat, and aids.

Ready to try? As you read, keep checking the five diagrams on pages 97 to 101. Also …

Before You Start

… run down my checklist to confirm that your horse is ready for this work.

■ **Get his attention.** Make sure he listens and responds to your outside leg aid. Check that these three

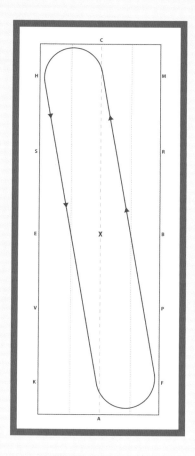

gymnastics are solid: **canter/trot/canter transitions** (so he remembers that when your outside leg is back from the hip, he continues cantering no matter what); **turn on the forehand in half-pass position** (to confirm that he listens and responds to your outside leg); and **three-loop serpentine with no change of bend** (if you and he can't stay counterbent and balanced at the trot, the canter will be a disaster).

■ **Get him comfortable.** Make sure he's comfortable and balanced cantering half a 10-meter circle. While doing my five steps, he's going to have to canter from the centerline onto the rail and from the rail onto the centerline.

■ **Plan for success.** Counter-canter doesn't have to be a big deal, but it is something new and challenging, so all conditions should be favorable. If, say, a gale is blowing, or you're out of sorts because you've had a bad day at

work, or your horse is distracted because it's feeding time, put these exercises on hold for today, and do them another time.

Step 1: The "Paper Clip"

The first requirement for counter-canter (and any movement) is that your horse stays straight. If he's like most horses, that's not a challenge while he's cantering on the rail or even on a track that's parallel to the rail, such as the centerline. Likewise, he's comfortable staying straight (in other words, aligned) cantering a circle. But ask him to stay straight on a non-parallel track, such as you often have to follow for counter-canter, and—believe me, I've seen this happen even with "trained" dressage horses from Europe—he panics, gets crooked, falls right, falls left, and stops listening to your seat and aids.

My "paper clip" solves that problem by introducing two angled tracks where you have almost the whole length of the arena to school and fix your horse. And by simply turning when you get to the end, you continue cantering without interruption—something you can't do when cantering a regular KXM diagonal, say. (When I'm riding a young horse, in fact, I perfect the paper clip before I ask him to canter across the diagonal.)

Pick up a left-lead canter on the rail. Carry your whip in your outside (right) hand so it's there, ready to reinforce your outside leg aid if necessary. Sit on your inside (left) seat bone, with your outside (right) leg back from the hip, and maintain an active, rhythmic swing in your seat. (You should feel as if your outside hip is pushing your inside hip forward.)

Keep enough contact to maintain a slight flexion to the left—just enough for you to see your horse's left eyelash—and to be able to half-halt on your outside (right) rein. Check that he's straight, with his inside hip aligned behind his inside shoulder.

Canter through the short side, past C, and at H turn onto a slightly angled track that aims at A. Now, this is important: As you ride toward A, keep your outside leg back so your horse continues cantering. Stay deep on your inside (left) seat bone. And keep your head, shoulders, and hips absolutely perpendicular to the track—so that if laser beams were shooting out of them, they'd shine on A. As you approach A, allow yourself enough room to ride a comfortable 10-meter half-circle so you end up on the rail near F, where you can begin another angled track toward C.

Keep going! This is not an exercise that you do once

Step 2

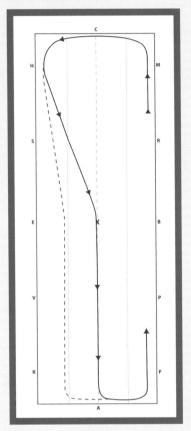

Step 3

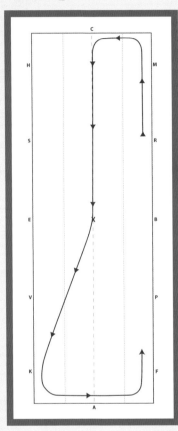

Step 2:
Turning off the H-to-X diagonal to the centerline on the left lead (solid line), you'll have about two easy strides of counter-canter. To make this step even more doable, ride the shallow dotted diagonal to the quarterline first.

Step 3:
It's trickier turning off the centerline and cantering back to the rail, which is why we do it next. The key is to maintain your horse's balance and your position so you don't leg-yield.

Step 4:
Join the diagonal lines together and you'll be riding a shallow counter-canter serpentine (solid line). Make the exercise doable by breaking it down (dotted line): Ride the diagonal, turn onto the quarter-line, ride about four straight strides, turn onto the next diagonal.

or twice and then have to drop so you don't blow your horse's mind. Not only can you do it repeatedly, just as if you were cantering around on the rail, but he needs the repetition to start understanding the pattern.

The very first time, your horse is going to wander like a lost soul. After a few times around, though, he's going to say, "Aha! I know what we're doing!" At that point, let it go; maybe do a few other gymnastics. Then ride the paper clip to the right. When he tells you that he gets it going that way, too, quit for the day.

The next time you try the paper clip, your horse will probably be a little lost again at first, but soon—sooner than last time—he'll say, "Ahhh ... now I remember." At that point, let it go again.

Mastering the paper clip could take a week, three

weeks, or a month. Don't get in a hurry. Stay with it until you feel as one with your horse, and until the track is as easy and predictable as if you were cantering the long side.

Step 2: Diagonal Line to Centerline
We know your horse is confident riding a centerline. By now he's also confident riding a diagonal line. So in this step we're going to put the two together by having you canter from H to X to A, where you'll turn left. What about the counter-canter? Your slight turn from the diagonal line onto the centerline will call for about two strides of counter-canter. (To make this step SUPER doable, first ride a very shallow diagonal to the near quarterline and then ride up the quarterline. Gradually move the track toward X.)

Step 4

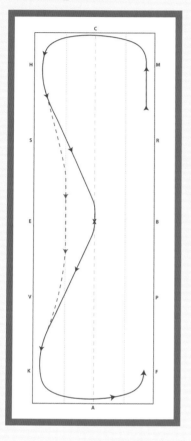

Pick up a left-lead canter, come through the short side, and at H turn toward X. Now, here's the key: About two strides before X, use about one stride when your horse's forehand is in the air to smoothly turn your head, shoulders, and hips so they're looking straight up the centerline at C. Change nothing else about your position! Continue to sit deep on your inside (left) seat bone, maintain a slight flexion left with your left hand, and half-halt by squeezing your right shoulder back and down. And guess what? In about two strides, your horse will smoothly bring his body around to catch up with your position—and in those two strides he will have been counter-cantering.

You'll now be cantering straight down the centerline, and you will have arrived there with no muss, no fuss, no problems. When you arrive at A, turn left and either canter all the way around the arena to start the pattern again at H or, if you feel prepared, repeat the pattern from F to X to C.

Repeat this step, a couple of times on each lead, several times a week. Again, you may need a couple of weeks to get it solid; if you have to school it two or three times before it feels good, your horse isn't yet ready to move on. But when you can just pull it out of your hat and he says, "Bingo! I got it," you're ready for …

Step 3: Centerline to Diagonal Line

Now we're going to ask your horse for two strides of counter-canter as he turns off the centerline onto a diagonal track back toward the rail, a step that's a bit trickier than Step 2. As you do this, for some reason—perhaps because you're turning back toward the rail, which seems to exert a magnetic pull—you're likely to let him change his balance, bulge into his outside right shoulder and do more of a leg-yield than a counter-canter. If you do let him, neither you nor he will be perpendicular to the diagonal track, and his haunches will no longer be following his shoulders. The key, there-fore, is that you really focus on your rider position.

Turn down the centerline at C. About two strides before X, use about one stride when your horse's fore-hand is in the air to smoothly turn your head, shoulders, and hips to the right so they're looking straight toward the letter K. Change nothing else about your position, and in the next couple of strides—counter-canter strides, not leg-yield strides—he should match your rider position. He'll smoothly turn onto the new diagonal track with his chest looking at K and his haunches following his shoul-ders. And that's all there is to it!

Continue to K, come through the short end, canter up to C, and begin again; or, if you feel prepared, turn up the centerline at A and ride A to X to M.

Again, when you can pull this step out of your hat, you're ready for …

Step 4: Diagonal Line to Centerline to Diagonal Line

You now have all the pieces of counter-canter in its most basic form; you and your horse should feel pretty confi-dent about putting them together. But again you'll school for success by making this step as doable as possible.

You want to end up riding two diagonals with about four straight strides, centered over X. To get there, you'll

(Continued on page 102)

STEP 5: The First-Level Loop

This shallow serpentine figure goes from the corner to X and back to the corner. Rather than make a sharp turn at X, I tell my students to ride a straight stride or two over X on the centerline. From a bird's-eye view, the track would look like a tire that's a little low on air; from the judge's perspective, it's a clear, precise, continuous curve.

1 We start the figure with Picasso cantering on the left lead, on the diagonal toward X. Even though we're going to make a shallow loop, the track is as arrow-straight as if I were riding the paper-clip pattern. I'm also keeping him straight through his body, with his inside hip and shoulder aligned, by keeping my head, hips, and shoulders perpendicular to the track. I'm sitting deep on my inside left seat bone, my inside leg at the girth and my outside leg slightly back from the hip. My whip is in my outside hand (in case he needs a tap to remind him that when my outside leg is back, it means "canter"). I have a little inside (left) flexion—just enough to see the eyelash of his left eye.

2 As we approach the centerline, I start rhythmically using a slightly stronger outside (right) leg and stronger pushes in my seat to make sure Picasso's haunches continue following his shoulders through the upcoming little counter-canter loop of the pattern. You can see that I'm not just sitting dead in the saddle; my seat is actively and rhythmically swinging with each stride.

3 In the next moment, with Picasso's body still on the diagonal line and his forehand in the air—on the up beat—I smoothly turn my hips, shoulders, and head so they're perpendicular to the new imaginary track up the centerline. My outside (right) leg is still back, I'm still deep on my inside (left) seat bone—and even though I'm asking him to change his track, my hands are quiet and exactly level with each other, and my shoulders, hips, and heels are perfectly aligned. This is the way a true canter looks; it's the way counter-canter should look.

4 And without any disruption in his balance or straightness, Picasso matches my rider position. Both my seat and his chest are perpendicular to the new track up centerline, and I've momentarily softened my outside leg and the swing in my seat because he's following me with a slight flexion to the left and his haunches right behind his shoulders.

5 In the next stride, when Picasso's forehand is once again in the air, I turn my head, shoulders, and hips—this time off the centerline and onto the new diagonal line.

6 And again, he follows my rider position, so we're both heading diagonally straight back to the rail.

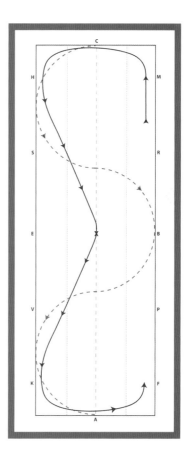

STEP 5

Here's the First Level counter-canter "loop" as I tell my students to ride it (solid line) as if it's a tire that's just a little low on air, which gives them one or two straight strides on the centerline, while the figure looks like a smooth, continuous curve. Once this feels comfortable, stretch the loops more and more until you're riding a full three-loop serpentine (dotted line).

start by coming across the diagonal at H and turning onto the quarterline when you're just about opposite S. Ride down the quarterline to a point that's opposite V; then ride a diagonal back to the rail at K.

When this pattern feels solid, you can gradually begin moving the track toward X, lengthening your diagonal lines and shortening your straight sections as you go. When the diagonal/centerline/diagonal sequence feels good, you're ready for …

Step 5: The First Level Counter-Canter Loop

The key to this step (which looks like one continuous curving line), I tell my students, is to make a track like a tire that's just a little low on air, so that they ride one or maybe two strides almost straight on the centerline. Believe me, ride it that way and not only will the track come out looking like one smooth, continuous curve, the entire figure will just be very clear, precise, and confident. Once this loop feels good, you can start increasing the difficulty by gradually going to the next quarterline and eventually to the rail. When you can do a true three-loop counter-canter serpentine, you're ready to come across the diagonal and counter-canter the short side. (For now, ride it as half a 20-meter circle.)

When your horse can do that, you're ready to start incorporating other gymnastic patterns. Do forward and back in counter-canter so you know he's really in front of your leg. And if you REALLY want a rub-your-tummy/pat-your-head exercise, try spiraling in and out on a 20-meter counter-canter circle. It's a mind-bender—but boy, will you prove that your horse is balanced, supple, and listening!

What If …

- **He breaks.** Your horse breaks from the left-lead canter to the trot? This rarely happens with my step-by-step system—but if it does, immediately quit the pattern and turn or circle back toward the left. (One of the beauties of these patterns is that you can always circle back in the direction of the lead you were on.)

  Reorganize and then do several trot/canter/trot transitions to remind him that when your outside leg is back, he canters, and that he keeps cantering until you bring your leg forward. Then go back and try the pattern again.

- **He changes leads.** Your horse grabs the bit, speeds up, and does a flying change from left to right? Walk, then circle left. Check your position—you may have let your outside (right) leg slip forward. Check to make sure you're keeping an inside (left) flexion and not letting your horse look right. If he's a hunter who automatically changes lead when he changes direction, exaggerate your aids a bit: Take a little more flexion to the left. Sit deeper on your inside (left) seat bone. Keep your outside (right) leg a bit farther back. And, again, reinforce your canter aids with trot/canter/trot transitions and forward and back (which tells him that stronger seat and leg aids don't necessarily mean "flying change"). When he feels as if he's listening, come again.

WRONG!

Cantering on the left lead, I'm making a classic mistake as I try to return to the track from the centerline. Instead of turning my head, shoulders, and hips to the right to tell Picasso where to go, I'm sitting perpendicular to the centerline, I'm tipping my upper body to the left, my seat is off to the right, and I'm squeezing with my left leg.

Nothing in my body language is telling him to go straight back to the rail; everything is telling him I want something closer to a very bad, very unbalanced leg-yield.

Picasso's chest is looking straight down the arena, his haunches are trailing his forehand, and it's clear that I've pulled his mildly protesting raised head so far left that all his weight is falling onto his right shoulder.

CHAPTER 15

GYMNASTIC EXERCISE 15: SHOULDER-IN

Here's a clear introduction to the first of the lateral movements.

I'm asking Cassiano to complete the 10-meter circle by getting him to lift his outside shoulder up and in, while engaging his left inside leg. On the completion of the circle the following stride will be shoulder-in.

I N CHAPTER 10, WHEN I INTRODUCED Gymnastic Pattern 10 (leg-yielding to and from the rail), I told you that one of the leg-yield's many benefits was the sturdy foundation it would lay for the lateral movements of shoulder-in, travers (haunches-in), renvers (haunches-out), and half-pass.

Leg-yield itself, I explained, wasn't technically a lateral movement, even though your horse would be moving sideways as well as forward. The distinction? In leg-yield, he stays straight from poll to tail. For a true lateral movement, his body bends evenly from poll to tail around your inside leg.

Well, that even bending through the body is what you're going to teach your horse here, with shoulder-in. In this gymnastic, his outside shoulder comes in off the track and aligns with his inside hind leg so he's on what we call "three tracks."

If you watched him coming toward you, you'd see his outside hind, his outside fore directly in front of his inside hind, and his inside fore. (When you can see all

four legs evenly spaced, by the way, he's said to be traveling on "four tracks," as he does in the "baby" shoulder-in called shoulder-fore, and in travers, renvers, and half-pass.)

It's Not Called "Dr. Shoulder-in" for Nothing

Shoulder-in as a test movement isn't required until Second Level in dressage. But I usually introduce it earlier, when my horses are stepping up from Training to First Level. If you've been following my gymnastic exercises up to this point, whether you do dressage or your

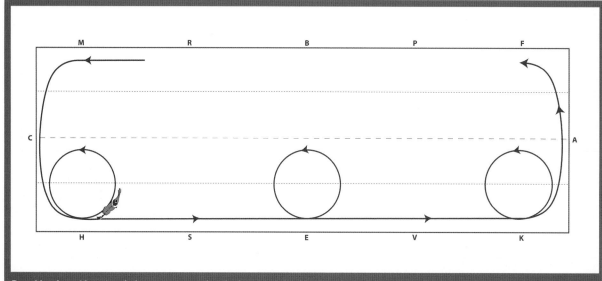

By asking for a 10-meter circle, we are preparing the horse to bring his shoulders off the rail. On the completion of the circle, the next stride will be the shoulder-in, followed by another 10-meter circle.

horse is a hunter, eq horse, jumper, or eventer, you can and should introduce it, too. That's because it's a useful (some say the most useful) gymnastic that …

■ Supples your horse and enhances his elasticity and freedom of movement all the way from shoulders to hindquarters.

■ Strengthens him and increases his engagement by getting him to lift his shoulders in front, and to step farther under himself and carry more weight behind.

■ Straightens him and improves his obedience to your aids by getting him to move more from your inside driving leg to your outside half-halting rein.

■ Prepares him not only for the rest of the lateral exercises, but for such upper-level movements as canter pirouettes and such on-course efforts as tight or rollback turns, balanced corners, and jumps that are close to a corner.

■ Saves your bacon! Shoulder-in is the most absolutely wonderful tool when your horse wants to spook. From the saddle, you cannot physically pull him past a scary object. But when you gain control over his shoulders, you can push him. Say he's young or green, he's at his first show, and he absolutely doesn't want to trot up centerline toward the scary-looking judge's stand. Just put him in a shoulder-fore. The judge won't care. In fact, she'll probably say, "Hah! What a smart rider! A little

shoulder-in is going to get her past this trouble spot without a fight."

Shoulder-in is also a lifesaver if you're on a young horse that wants to start bucking: If he's in shoulder-in, he can't buck! At that point, even if it's not the world's most correct shoulder-in, who cares? You're keeping a dangerous situation from developing.

Shoulder-in Prerequisites

Here are the tools you need to succeed:

■ All the gymnastic exercises leading up to this one, especially forward and back, turn on the forehand in leg-yield position, leg-yield itself, spiral-in and -out, even counter-canter, (so you recall the feel of making a subtle but critical adjustment to your rider position).

■ Sitting trot, because you'll have complete control over your horse's up- and down-beat. If, however, sitting the trot gives you so much difficulty that it upsets your position or makes his job harder, by all means post.

■ A new rider position. Ever since we began I've been telling you that your hips and shoulders should always be perpendicular to the track. Well, now is one of the few times when you're going to keep them parallel to the track by making them un-parallel to each other. Let me explain: In shoulder-in, your horse's haunches are going

Start With Leg-Yield on the Rail

The best way to show a horse he can travel straight down the rail with his haunches on the track and his shoulders off is with a movement he already knows: leg-yield. But instead of asking Cassiano to move diagonally across the arena while staying straight through his body and parallel to the rail, I'm asking him to stay straight through his body but to move parallel to the rail and at an angle to the track.

I set him up by riding a 20-meter circle, which required almost no bend through his body. As I approached the rail in the corner, I asked for a few steps of spiral-out—with the feel of pushing his haunches further out than his forehand—to position him on about a 40- to 45-degree angle to the rail, but straight through his body, with his outside shoulder and hip aligned, and clearly on four tracks.

Now I'm just asking him to continue straight down the rail, rhythmically squeezing my inside (left) leg on the up-beat—when his inside hind and outside fore are in flight. In the same moment, a squeeze from my outside (right) half-halting rein raises and "pauses" his outside fore and holds him in case he wants to bulge or lean into his right shoulder.

My inside (left) rein maintains just enough flexion that I see his left eyelash. And my outside (right) leg is a hair behind my inside leg and fairly passive: Even if Cassiano wants to move his haunches a little too much to the rail, as long as he maintains his

forward energy and stays straight from poll to tail, it's kind of what I want him to do! My shoulders are square and perpendicular to the angled track, and my hips are shooting light beams straight out on either side of his neck on an angle into the arena, where I want his haunches looking.

If he starts to overbend, slow, or lose this angle, I'll circle 20 meters, then start over. At the end of the arena, I'll circle 20 meters before straightening him and continuing around on the rail.

to travel straight down the long side, but his forehand is going to come in on about a 30-degree angle.

Because your hips, thighs, and the upper part of your calves control his hindquarters, that part of your body has to continue facing down the long side, perpendicular to the rail. But because your torso and shoulders influence and control his forehand, they have to turn slightly and face into the arena.

Try it right now as you're sitting there reading. I'm going to talk you through a shoulder-in left, so we'll go that way: Put your elbows by your sides and your fists closed in front of you as if holding the reins. Keep your seat straight and square in your chair (think "laser beams are shooting straight ahead out of my hips") while you very subtly turn your upper body about 30 degrees: not with a big twisting or tipping, but by staying perfectly level as you bring your left shoulder and upper arm back a bit and your right shoulder and upper arm a bit forward. What to do with your head? It must match your shoulders, but with your eyes still looking down the long side where you're going. Got it? Great!

■ Leg-yield on the rail. (For how, check out the photo above). When leg-yield on the rail feels dependable and comfortable in both directions, you're ready to …

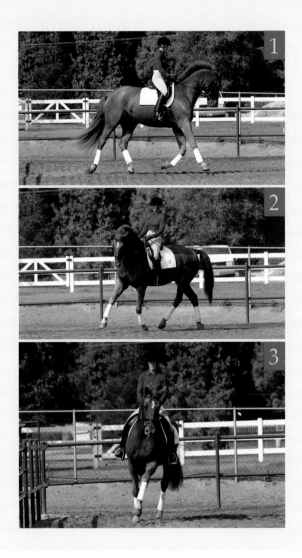

Prepare With a 10-Meter Circle

1 Before asking for a shoulder-in left on the rail, I ride a 10-meter circle in the corner to establish the even poll-to-tail bend Cassiano will need. I'm carrying my whip on the inside because my inside leg aid is going to be the dominant one; I want my whip right there to touch or tap him if my leg needs a bit of reinforcement. For the moment, though, he's nicely forward and energetic. I'm sitting square and still, with my outside leg a bit back, weight in my heel, and my hips and shoulders perpendicular to the 10-meter circular track. And I'm starting to look for the feeling that when I half-halt my outside (right) rein on the up-beat—when his inside hind and outside fore are in flight—he responds by bringing his outside fore up and around, almost as if …

2 … he's creating the bend in his shoulder by crossing his outside fore in front of his inside fore.

3 And here we are on the down-beat of the last stride of the circle: I'm still sitting perpendicular to the circular track, my hips and shoulders looking where his chest is looking, my outside leg still back. In the next step, the moment his inside fore and outside hind touch down and he starts the up-beat, I'll change my rider position. My hips will look down the long side to tell his haunches to go straight, while my shoulders will look into the ring on about the 30-degree angle I want his shoulders to assume— almost as if his forehand is staying on the circle for one more stride. And with that, we'll be in shoulder-in.

Ride a Shoulder-In

Tracking left, pick up an energetic sitting trot. When your horse is listening and light in your hand, which means he's elevated in his shoulders and actively using his hind end, come around the short side of the arena. As soon as you've come through the second corner onto the long side, immediately ride a 10-meter circle. Sit deeper on your inside (left) seat bone, with your inside leg at the girth, your outside leg a hair behind it, and your hips and shoulders perpendicular to the track.

You NEVER want this to feel as if you're pulling him around with your inside (left) rein. Instead, it's very much like a spiral-in. Every time his inside hind leg and outside

fore start to leave the ground, bring his shoulder just a tiny bit in by pressing with your outside leg and giving a strong inward half-halt (as you squeeze your outside shoulder back and down, bring your outside rein against his neck to almost push against his shoulder). The feeling you're after: Instead of reaching straight out in front, his outside fore comes up and around so he's shaping the circular track.

As you come around on the last strides of the circle and start to feel his shoulders approaching the track on the long side, continue asking him to circle. In the next stride, when he's almost straight on the track, continue to say "Circle." But in the next stride, when you feel as if

Shoulder-In

1 After riding a 10-meter circle and asking for shoulder-in, I may have Cassiano a hair over-angled, but he's still evenly and correctly bent from poll to tail: His nose is at the point of his shoulder; if he had not just brought his outside fore in before setting it down, he'd be traveling on three aligned tracks. I'm not trying to pull his shoulders in. I'm shaping him by keeping my inside leg rhythmically strong at the girth, taking a slight indirect rein on the inside, keeping my outside leg back, and creating an "inside leg to outside rein" connection by maintaining a half-halting contact on my outside rein. (Here's a helpful trick: I'm using the shadow my arena fence casts to keep Cassiano's track down the rail straight.)

2 On the up-beat, Cassiano is aligned on three tracks. I'm half-halting on my outside rein, sitting deeper on my inside seat bone, and driving strongly with my inside seat and leg. I'm also shooting those light beams out of my hips, straight down the track, while my shoulders continue to look to the inside.

3 In the next step, on the down-beat—note that his outside fore is once again a hair past his inside hind—I soften my outside half-halting rein but continue to hold him fairly strongly with my inside leg.

4 And in the next step of the up-beat, I again bring my outside shoulder back and down to half-halt on the outside rein, asking Cassiano to pause and hover his outside fore and bring it a bit more …

5 … to the inside as my strong inside driving leg and my rider position—hips looking straight down the rail—keep his haunches continuing straight, so he stays in shoulder-in and doesn't circle.

If I Lose the Bend

… and I can't re-create it within one stride by using a little more indirect rein, sitting a little deeper on my inside seat bone, and pushing more strongly with my inside leg, I immediately circle 10 meters. I relax my inside indirect rein and my inside leg, turn my seat so it's again parallel to my shoulders and perpendicular to the 10-meter circular track—and Cassiano circles! As we come back around toward the rail, I'll repeat the process of setting him up for a shoulder-in.

shoulder-in is to lean on his inside shoulder. That extra little bit of indirect left rein throws just a penny's worth more weight onto his right shoulder—his outside shoulder—which will really make him engage, sit down, and get more expressive with his inside hind.)

Encourage your horse's shoulder to come off the track and stay off by turning your chest and shoulders toward the arena on about a 30-degree angle. And tell his haunches to continue straight down the long side by directing laser beams out of your hips and straight down the track. On each up-beat, when his inside hind and outside fore are in flight, strongly squeeze your inside leg at the girth, almost with the feeling that you're pushing your inside hip toward his outside shoulder and down the track.

After three to five strides—your horse won't be able to hold the bend longer than that at first—ride another 10-meter circle. He already has his forehand off the rail, even if he's lost a little bend; so just relax your inside leg, soften your inside indirect rein, smoothly bring your hips around so they're once again parallel to your shoulders and perpendicular to the circular track, and—boom! Just like that, you're circling!

As you return to the rail, repeat the aids for shoulder-in: Think, "We're going to circle again"—but the moment your horse's shoulders come away from the track and both your chest and his are facing into the arena, turn your hips so they're facing down the long side, take an indirect inside rein, add a very strong inside leg, and continue in shoulder-in to the end of the arena.

This is important. On a young horse, or on one who's just learning shoulder-in, I never get to the end of the long side and simply straighten him by bringing his shoulders back onto the track in front of his haunches. Instead, I ride one more 10-meter circle in the corner because it reestablishes any balance or bend he may have lost and reinforces the idea of bringing his shoulder up and in. (I begin or finish shoulder-in without circling only when he can stay balanced, expressive, and almost perfect in shoulder-in all the way down the long side.)

he'd make another circle if you kept going, ask him for a shoulder-in down the long side instead: At the very moment he's bringing his outside shoulder up and in for another stride of circle, take a little bit of an indirect inside rein—not by pulling, but by turning the knuckles of your left hand toward your right hip. (One of the first and biggest mistakes a horse will attempt to make in

Make It Even MORE Gymnastic

When you're comfortably going the full length of the arena in shoulder-in, increase the difficulty by asking your horse for some forward and back in shoulder-in. But the first few times you ask be ready—with a clear indirect rein and strong leg on the inside, and with a good half-halting rein on the outside—for him to say "OK" but then try to straighten his body.

Ride shoulder-in on a circle (and when that's good, try adding in some forward and back, too). Try a shoulder-in spiral-in and spiral-out. Or here's a challenging exercise that my mentor, Erich Bubbel, taught me: Stay in shoulder-in left the entire time you ride from F to B, turn left at B, turn left at E, and ride from E to K.

What if ...

■ **Tail-end trouble.** You feel your horse trying to throw his haunches out rather than bring his shoulders in? Hold his haunches with a stronger outside leg.

■ **His head goes but his shoulders don't.** His shoulders stay on the track and only his head and neck come in? Make sure you're not just pulling his head and neck around (as I'm doing in the "wrong" photo below). Then take a step back and review the easier movement of leg-yield on the rail (see the photo on page 105), to remind him that his shoulders can come in while his haunches stay out.

■ **He loses alignment.** Your horse loses his even bend from poll to tail and so develops too much angle? Check to make sure your inside hand is looking toward your outside hip; then immediately circle 10 meters to restore the correct bend from poll to tail, and to remind him about bringing his outside fore up and in.

■ **His speed sags.** Your horse gets slower and slower? This is such a common problem that I've never known a horse to become more forward while learning shoulder-in. (In fact, if you know one, I'd like to meet him!) That said, I am OK with your horse's slowing down a little bit to figure out the movement, but not so much that he falls behind your leg and the movement becomes more difficult. If that happens, just circle and refresh him with some "forward," even if you have to post the trot or ride a bigger 12- or even 15-meter circle. Remember he must always respond by going forward.

WRONG!

I've pulled Cassiano's head and neck so far to the left that his nose is past the point of his shoulder: a real no-no at any time. As a result, he can't bring his shoulders in off the rail. Instead, he's leaning on his outside (right) shoulder, his chest is looking straight up the track, and he's even a little bit haunches-in! You can also see that my rider position isn't helping: My hips are looking straight down the track, but so are my shoulders.

CHAPTER 16

GYMNASTIC EXERCISE 16: HAUNCHES-IN & HALF-PASS

They supple, strengthen, and balance your horse. And guess what: If you learn the one, the other will be a piece of cake!

The way I'm going to teach you to ride half-pass, it's nothing more than haunches-in on the diagonal.

I N THIS, OUR FINAL CHAPTER, WE'LL WRAP UP my series of gymnastic exercises. And we're doing it with two lateral movements: haunches-in (also known as travers) and half-pass.

In haunches-in, your horse does the opposite of shoulder-in (Chapter 15): He still moves down the long side of the arena, but his forehand is to the rail and his head and chest look where he's going. By virtue of an even bend around your inside leg, his hindquarters come to the inside. His body is on about a 30-degree angle to the rail.

If you were to stand in front of him, you'd see his legs on four evenly spaced tracks, with his outside legs passing and crossing in front of his inside legs. Haunches-in is the first lateral movement in which he has to look and move into the direction of travel.

In half-pass, your horse again stays bent around your inside leg and again moves into the direction of travel, with his outside legs passing and crossing in front of his inside legs. But instead of following the rail, he moves on a diagonal track across the arena. His body stays basically parallel to the long side (although his forehand is ever-so-slightly in advance of his hindquarters).

Why do I group these two gymnastic exercises together? Because the way I teach half-pass—one of the big bugaboo movements to many dressage riders—it's nothing more than haunches-in on the diagonal: Master the one and you've got the other!

For example, the other day I was giving a lesson to a new student, an event rider. He had shown me some leg-

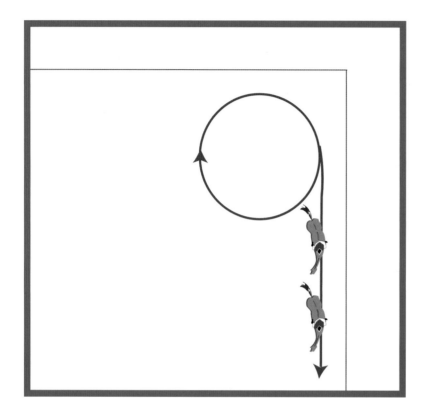

yield, shoulder-in, and haunches-in, so I asked him, "Have you ever done a half-pass?" And it was kind of cute, because he said, "I don't know." So I explained the movement, then told him to do one more haunches-in down the long side. As he finished the haunches-in and came through the short side of the arena, I told him to come across the diagonal doing the same thing—haunches-in—again. He did, and I yelled, "THAT is a half-pass!" His response? "Wow! That was easy!" It was fun for me to see it work so well, and it was fun for him to just kind of have it happen.

What's So Gymnastic About These Exercises?

If you're a dressage rider, you know that haunches-in and half-pass increase your horse's all-important engagement and collection. They also prepare him for walk and canter pirouettes. Haunches-in is required at Second Level; half-pass, at Third Level.

If you're a hunter/jumper rider, that

Haunches-in

1 Just as with the last chapter's shoulder-in, I established the correct bend through Cassiano's body on a 10-meter circle to the right. Now, as his left shoulder comes back to the track, but while his haunches are still finishing the circle—kind of like a circle minus a stride—I start to apply my haunches-in aids. I take a slight indirect inside (right) rein to establish a good inside flexion in his jowl. I'm sitting deep on my inside seat bone, and my shoulders and hips are looking to the outside of the arena, with my outside (left) leg a bit farther back than my left shoulder. At this moment, on the up beat of his outside hind, I press and drive with my outside leg to ask him to bring his outside hind forward and across toward his inside (right) shoulder and his inside flexion.

2 In the next step, Cassiano's in a very correct haunches-in. He's on four pretty evenly spaced tracks, and his chest is looking straight down the long side. I've relaxed my outside leg and now, with his inside hind and outside fore in flight, I'm half-halting on the outside rein and pressing and squeezing with my inside leg at the girth to say "C'mon! Come forward."

3 And now, in the next step, Cassiano is really bending his hock, engaging, and stepping under his body mass. I'm still sitting deep on my inside seat bone and keeping my upper body erect. The fact that I'm driving more strongly with my outside (left) leg doesn't mean that I sit to the outside or tip my body that way. (In fact, if I were to sit more heavily on my outside seat bone, I'd automatically force my horse to put more balance on his inside shoulder, no matter how much indirect rein I used.)

4 And here we are once again with the inside hind and outside fore coming forward, and nothing about Cassiano's angle, flexion, or position has changed. (The toe of my left boot tells you two things, by the way: My left foot tends to stick out more than my right because of an old skiing injury. And I'm clearly not bending my knee and raising my heel to push, drive, and ask him to bring his haunches in.)

Half-Pass

1 I prepare for half-pass by carrying my whip in my left hand in case my dominant half-pass leg needs support, and by riding across the MXK diagonal with Cassiano straight from poll to tail. My shoulders and hips are perpendicular to the diagonal line and looking at K. I have an inside (right) flexion in his jowl so my outside (left) half-halts go through.

When he flexes right that slightly increases the contact and influence of the bit on the left side of his mouth. But the flexion is so slight that his nose is still in the middle of his chest. If beams of light were shooting out of my hips, Cassiano's head would be in the middle between them.

2 As we cross the quarterline and Cassiano's outside (left) hind starts to come forward, I ask him for haunches-in: I take an indirect inside (right) rein.

Because his body in half-pass should be parallel to the rail, I turn my hips and shoulders to face the end of the arena, so my position is now perpendicular to the rail. And I move my outside (left) leg back and drive with it. In response, he brings his forehand around so his chest is perpendicular to the long side of the arena, starts to move his haunches right, and begins to bring his left hind leg under his body, toward his right shoulder. I call this "driving his outside hind into his inside flexion."

3 In the next step, I give a rhythmical squeeze with my inside (right) leg to remind Cassiano that he still has to come forward, and I half-halt on my outside rein to ask him to pause his outside fore and cross it over.

may seem like pretty heady stuff, but don't let it get you intimidated or put off. You and your horse can still do both patterns. You might not score very high with a dressage judge because your horse isn't super-collected, or maybe you have to post the trot to keep him going energetically forward, but he'll still have to bend around your inside leg, move into the direction of travel, and bring his outside leg more under his body. And that can't help but supple him, strengthen him, improve his balance, increase his carrying power behind, and increase his ability to understand and obey your aids.

Prerequisites for Haunches-in and Half-Pass

Review all my gymnastic exercises, but look especially at …
- **Softening the jaw.** See, too, the way an inside flexion gets your horse to place a penny's worth more balance on

4 And in the step after that, I again drive with my outside leg and Cassiano again steps forward and across. Without wiggling, tipping, or making any obvious moves, I'm doing a little bit of rhythmic "inside, outside, inside, outside" to make the half-pass happen. Does it work?

5 Here is the same movement, as seen from the end of the arena. Cassiano is slightly shoulder-fore, as he should be. He's bringing his outside hind forward and across, toward his right shoulder. He's well balanced, and although you can't see my inside indirect rein, you can see that he's flexed to the inside. I'm sitting on my inside (right) seat bone, and my position is perpendicular to the rail. In a few strides, as we cross the quarterline, I'll tell him to straighten and finish the diagonal by relaxing my indirect rein, bringing my left leg forward, and turning so my position is again facing the corner.

his outside shoulder (Chapter 3). Remember, in everything we do with a horse, he's always supposed to have a little more weight or balance on his outside shoulder.

■ **Three-loop serpentine with no change of bend.** Pay special mind to its preparation with turn on the forehand in half-pass position—where your horse started learning to move his haunches away from your outside driving leg (Chapter 9).

■ **Two tracks on a circle.** In this exercise you increased his maneuverability, straightness, and suppleness by moving his haunches to the inside at the walk (Chapter 13).

■ **Shoulder-in.** With this exercise he started learning the new skill of traveling down the rail with a part of him—his shoulders—to the inside (Chapter 15).

Some Thoughts About Your Aids

■ **Your leg aid:** From the beginning of this book I've stressed that when I say "leg," I'm talking about your entire leg, from your hip all the way down through your upper calf, with your toes looking straight ahead and your weight dropped down into your heel. Yet it seems that as soon as we come to lateral work, people start lifting their heels or lower legs to ask their horses to bend

Two Common Mistakes in Half-Pass

1 This is a typical rider-position mistake: I'm tilting my upper body and sitting on my outside seat bone in an effort to get Cassiano to half-pass. But I'm tilting so far that my inside (right) leg is off his side and I've dropped my left shoulder. In trying to push his haunches over, I've ended up with no bend through his body and his balance on his right shoulder.

2 And this is a typical error of execution: Because my rider position is looking to the left, I'm *not* driving Cassiano's outside hind toward his inside shoulder. Instead, I've committed the big no-no of pushing his haunches so far over that they're traveling in advance of his forehand, he's no longer parallel to the rail, and he's leaning on his inside shoulder. I won't be able to correct him without first fixing my position, turning my shoulders and hips straight so they're perpendicular to the long side.

or move sideways, to the point that their spurs almost poke up underneath their square saddle pads! It's unattractive; what's even worse, it's ineffective and weak.

Want proof about which kind of leg is stronger, more effective, and far more secure? Sitting on your horse, have a friend stand next to you and put her hand, palm facing out, between your upper calf (just below the knee) and your saddle. Now ask her to try to pull your leg away from the saddle while you "use" the leg. First do it by raising your heel or lower leg; I'll bet she'll easily pull your leg away.

Then roll your thigh in to establish a firm but relaxed continuous contact from your seat bone down through your knee and the upper part of your calf, with your toes pointing ahead and your heels down, and have her try again; I'll be surprised if pulling your leg away isn't much harder—maybe impossible. Now, you tell me which is the stronger leg aid.

■ **Your rein aid:** In Chapter 15 I told you that a slight inside indirect rein would help your shoulder-in by increasing your horse's flexion and making sure he kept his balance on his outside shoulder. Here I want to expand on that idea.

> By your consistently establishing an indirect rein when you do lateral work, BINGO! your horse will always know exactly what's coming.

Like such top trainers as Finland's Kyra Kyrklund, Spain's Juan Matute, and my late mentor Erich Bubbel, I do all lateral work—shoulder-in, haunches-in (travers), haunches-out (renvers), and half-pass—with an indirect rein. I don't make a big move. I never jerk or pull. And I never cross my inside hand over my horse's withers. Rather, I just flex my inside wrist enough to turn my knuckles a bit. Instead of directing the pressure and feel straight back toward my inside hip, I'm guiding it ever-so-slightly toward my outside hip.

Put down the book and try doing that right now: Hold your elbows at your sides and close your fingers on imaginary reins as if you're riding your horse straight ahead. Now flex your right wrist just enough to turn the second joints—the knuckles—of your fingers toward your left hip. As you can see, it's not much of a movement at all, but it's a powerful one that achieves three goals.

You'll make sure your horse maintains the inside flexion of his jowl. You'll make sure he keeps his balance on his outside shoulder (avoiding one of the biggest mistakes a horse can make in haunches-in and half-pass: to fall and lean on his inside shoulder). And you'll make your aids black and white, with no gray areas. By your consistently establishing an indirect rein when you do lateral work, BINGO! your horse will always know exactly what's coming.

Haunches-in

Pick up an energetic sitting trot, tracking right. When your horse is listening and light in your hand, come through the short side and—just as you did in the last chapter for shoulder-in—ride a 10-meter circle in the corner to establish the correct poll-to-tail bend for haunches-in. Sit deeper on your inside (right) seat bone, with your inside leg at the girth, your outside leg a hair behind your inside leg, and your hips and shoulders perpendicular to the circular track.

As you start to return to the rail, think, "With a circle minus a stride, my horse's forehand will end up on the rail, but his haunches will still be on the circle and so to the inside." The very moment his outside (left) shoulder touches the track and his outside hind and inside fore are about to come off the ground, use your body language and aids to ask for haunches-in: Take an inside (right) indirect rein by turning your right knuckles toward your left hip. Turn your seat and shoulders so the beams of light coming out of your hips are shooting outside the arena on about a 30-degree angle to the rail.

This will automatically make you sit deeper on your inside (right) seat bone and bring your outside leg farther back. Now press to drive strongly with your outside leg, telling your horse to keep his haunches to the inside and to bring his outside hind forward under his mass and across in front of his inside hind, toward his inside shoulder.

In the next moment, as his inside hind and outside fore start to leave the ground, relax your outside leg, half-halt on your outside rein, and squeeze at the girth with your inside leg to tell him, "Come forward."

Now here's the good news: With all the previous gymnastic exercises as foundation, haunches-in should click in easily and pretty fast. But if your horse gets confused, his balance goes funny, or he slows down, just relax your indirect rein and outside leg, turn your body back to the inside, and circle 10 meters to reestablish the bend. Then ask for haunches-in again. If you can get four to six consecutive strides without losing the angle or bend or slowing down, you should be thrilled. If you can get from the corner to the letter B with balance and forwardness, you're doing great! Circle at B, straighten up, pet him, and go forward.

When you can do a balanced, obedient, energetic haunches-in from one end of the arena to the other without circling, start adding in a little forward and back. When you can lengthen and collect in haunches-in on the long side, you're ready for haunches-in on the diagonal, otherwise known as …

Half-Pass

Pick up an energetic sitting trot tracking right, come around the short side, and ride the MXK diagonal straight a couple of times. (After doing shoulder-in and haunches-in for a while, you may find your horse is suddenly wandering all over the place. So make sure he can ride a straight diagonal again, with his haunches following his forehand.) Check that he's lively, engaged, and soft in the bridle, with his forehand elevated and no crookedness or leaning.

> Half-pass is one pattern in which you totally have to imagine a solid rail running from corner to corner along the diagonal line; your horse's outside shoulder is going to touch and move along that imaginary rail.

When your horse gives you that feeling, come across the diagonal again and do a half-pass. But do it this way: From the corner to about the first quarterline, ride absolutely straight, with your shoulders and hips looking straight at K. Now, this is important: Half-pass is one pattern in which you totally have to imagine a solid rail running from corner to corner along the diagonal line; your horse's outside (left) shoulder is going to touch and move along that imaginary rail. So as you cross the quarterline and his outside (left) hind and inside (right) fore are about to leave the ground, take a little indirect (right) rein. Turn your rider position so your shoulders and hips are perpendicular to the quarterline instead of to the diagonal.

Again, this will automatically make you sit deeper on your inside (right) seat bone and bring your outside (left)

leg farther back from the hip. What's more, because your horse is technically parallel to the long side in half-pass, your rider position has to be perpendicular to the long side as well. Press and drive with your outside leg; then, on the outside down beat, relax that outside leg, half-halt on your outside rein, and press and drive with your inside leg. It's a very rhythmical kind of thing, but it's very subtle. It all happens in split seconds, and it can't—shouldn't—be seen by the naked eye, but it should be felt by your horse.

As you cross the second quarterline, straighten your horse—because that's probably about all the half-pass he can hold at first. (Besides, if he gets to the corner in half-pass position, I promise, he'll bounce off the rail like a bumper car—and you don't want that.) So relax your indirect rein, turn your body so your hips and shoulders are facing K and your outside leg comes forward, and reestablish the feel of your inside leg driving to your outside rein when his inside hind and outside fore are in flight.

Make It MORE Gymnastic

As your horse gets stronger and understands the movement better, lengthen the distance he half-passes on the diagonal until you're half-passing rail-to-rail. Get into the half-pass by coming through the corner and starting to turn onto the diagonal line, but applying your half-pass aids—indirect rein, body perpendicular to the long side, dominant outside driving leg—before his haunches make the turn. At the other end of the diagonal, come onto the rail early, hold the right bend for a couple of steps, and—before the corner—straighten for a stride and change to the new left bend.

Ride a counter-bent 20-meter circle; then ask your horse to do spiral-in and spiral-out. When you spiral in, you'll use leg-yield aids, and he'll start to learn not to lean on his inside shoulder (which, of course, is to the outside of the pattern). When you spiral out, you'll use half-pass aids and simply … half-pass!

In or out, you'll feel "uh-oh, there go the shoulders" or "oops, there go the haunches," and in time you'll learn how to control him totally from nose to tail. But that's what makes this exercise so amazing: You'll finally experience his body as a whole, instead of in parts. And once you do that, you've got half-pass—and practically anything else you want to do with your horse. ■

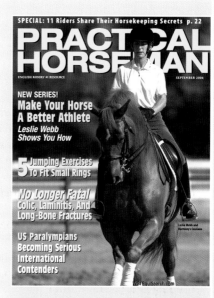
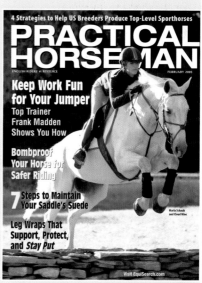
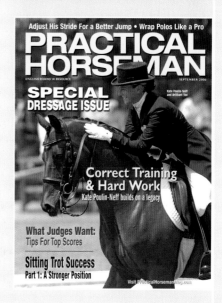